"Far too often, we parrot biblical words without really knowing what they mean. Dr. Crowe has given the church an excellent summary of what the Gospels mean by the phrase 'kingdom of God,' but he has also given us more—a practical handbook to understand how to read the Gospels well, seeing their central point, Jesus Christ and His kingdom. Highly recommended for both church leaders and laity who want to know the Gospels more deeply."

—Dr. William B. Fullilove
Professor of Old Testament
Reformed Theological Seminary

"The Gospels sum up Jesus' preaching: 'The kingdom of God has drawn near. Repent, and believe the good news.' The coming of God's kingdom was the heart of Jesus' message, and it was the purpose of His mission. God's eternal Son entered human history as the messianic Son, the royal Rescuer promised to Israel and the hope of salvation for all peoples. Exploring both the Gospels and the whole New Testament (with its Old Testament backstory), *The Kingdom of God and the Work of Christ* traces the tapestry that interweaves the kingdom's paradoxical power with the King's identity and redemptive achievement. This study is clear, concise, and comprehensive—a challenging blend to achieve for so rich a theme! Moreover, it is convicting: each chapter concludes with 'practical takeaways' that challenge us to trust humbly and submit eagerly to the King who has come and who reigns today at God's right hand."

—Dr. Dennis E. Johnson
Emeritus Professor of Practical Theology
Westminster Seminary California

"The gospel of the kingdom of God stands at the center of the Scriptures and at the heart of the Christian faith. This gospel is, however, often misunderstood. In *The Kingdom of God and the Work of Christ*, Brandon Crowe provides a sure guide to this crucial topic. He shows from the four Gospels that God's saving kingdom was promised in the Old Testament, was inaugurated by Jesus' life, death, and resurrection, and will reach its consummation when Jesus returns. In God's kingdom, sinners find forgiveness, enemies become citizens, God's people find fullness of life, and God Himself is glorified. This is good news indeed! Whether you are new to the topic, or coming to it again afresh, you will find here treasure both new and old (Matt. 13:52)."

—Dr. Murray Smith
Lecturer in Biblical Theology and Exegesis
Christ College, Australia

The Kingdom of God and the Work of Christ

The Kingdom of God and the Work of Christ

BRANDON D. CROWE

Ligonier Ministries

The Kingdom of God and the Work of Christ

Published by Ligonier Ministries
421 Ligonier Court, Sanford, FL 32771
Ligonier.org

Printed in China
Dream Colour
0001225
First printing

ISBN 978-1-64289-743-2 (Hardcover)
ISBN 978-1-64289-744-9 (ePub)

Cover design: Ligonier Creative
Interior design and typeset: Ligonier Editorial

Library of Congress Control Number: 2025946170

For Cherilyn and Brian

Contents

Preface ... xi

1 The Kingdom and the Four Gospels ... 1

2 The Context for the Kingdom ... 17

3 The True King Arrives ... 33

4 The Gospel of the Kingdom ... 47

5 The Timing of the Kingdom ... 61

6 The Signs of the Kingdom ... 71

7 The Clash of Kingdoms ... 83

8 The Parables of the Kingdom ... 97

9 The Ethics of the Kingdom ... 113

10 The Reversal of Worldly Standards ... 127

11 The People of the Kingdom ... 135

12 The Kingdom of the Suffering Messiah ... 151

13 The Greater David ... 161

14 The Death of the King ... 171

15 The Resurrection and the Spread of the Kingdom.......... 183
16 The Kingdom Today.. 195
For Further Reading.. 203
Scripture Index.. 205
About the Author... 213

Preface

The kingdom of God has been widely invoked in the modern world, but I suspect that it has been widely misunderstood. This book looks particularly at the Gospels to understand the message of Jesus about the kingdom of God (and the kingdom of heaven). The kingdom is crucial to Jesus' teaching, and it's therefore crucial that we understand it faithfully. Since the kingdom is closely related to the gospel message, this is also a book about how the gospel message is found in the four Gospels.

My primary focus in what follows is to address this question: What is the meaning of the kingdom of God in the Gospels, and how does this relate to Christ and what He has done for us? I give most attention to explaining Gospel texts, especially in the light of the Old Testament. I also include practical points at the end of each chapter, though readers may think of other application points in addition to these.

Thanks to Aaron Garriott for the invitation to write this volume and to everyone behind the scenes who helped this book see the light of day. I have benefited over the years as a professor of courses on the Gospels, where much of this material has been taught and engaged by capable students. I received helpful feedback from James Beevers, Caleb Burkhart, Iain Duguid, and Jonny Gibson. A special thanks to my wife for all she does to love and serve our family. I dedicate this book to my sister and brother-in-law, with the hope that it will be of use to them as they seek to live faithful, kingdom-centered lives in their various callings.

1

The Kingdom and the Four Gospels

When I was a child, my grandfather had on his mantel a small piece of wood shaped like a tiny porch with a roof. Underneath that roof were two small nails. He asked me if I knew what it was. I didn't. He would chuckle and say, "It's a 'tacks shelter.'" I was supposed to find this funny, but I had no idea what he was talking about. I didn't know what a tax shelter was, so I didn't know why "tacks shelter" was such a clever joke.

Sometimes trying to understand the Bible is like this. We come across a term or a concept, and we nod as though we know what it means, but we really don't. I was a college student when I realized one day that I didn't know what Jesus meant by "the kingdom of God." At this point, I was familiar with the Gospels and had read them many times. But honestly, I didn't know how to explain the kingdom of God. I had a vague idea, but I shuffled past the phrase without really digging down into it. I was comfortable with a vague idea of what it probably meant, but I would not have been able to articulate a thorough definition. I had the same lingering question in my early days of seminary. It wasn't until I began to learn from class and reading about the kingdom that I started to feel confident in my understanding of it. It was one of those topics that I didn't understand as well as I needed to.

What about you? Regardless of how much or how little you've read the Bible, do you really understand what Jesus means by "the kingdom"? Do you labor over it? Do you perhaps read right past it? Do you intuit the meaning from context? Does it refer to the church? To a principle for how we live? To some future reality?

How about the phrase *kingdom of heaven*? Is this the same thing as the kingdom of God? Does it simply mean "heaven"? Or something else?

These are not trivial questions. The kingdom was central to the teaching of Jesus in the Gospels, and we need to be sure we're interpreting this concept well if we want to interpret the Gospels well.

Since this is such a key concept in the Gospels, as its frequency indicates, it will not do to shuffle past or skim over something so central to the message of Jesus. Everything Jesus said is important. We can be doubly sure that repeated elements in His teaching are worthy of our study and reflection.

Jesus did not explain where the concept of the kingdom came from. But this is because it was so commonly understood that its background would have been obvious to the original audience. The same may not be true for us today. Therefore, we need to consider its background to appreciate what Jesus meant by the phrasing.

Yet in another sense, Jesus explained what the kingdom is every time He mentioned the concept. Though He wasn't the first to speak about the kingdom, He recalibrated and redefined what many people expected the kingdom of God to be. Jesus' teaching and His kingdom are full of surprises.

Back to my question: How would you define the kingdom of God? This is not an insignificant question; it relates quite centrally to what you believe about theology and the gospel message. It makes a big difference. Getting this right will help us stay oriented to theological true north; getting this wrong threatens to lead us off the straight path into a theological ditch.

So I invite you on the journey of this book. If you do not know what Jesus meant by "the kingdom of God," this is a good place to start. If you think you have some idea, then I hope to help you gain more clarity in your understanding. And even if you're already confident you know what it means, I hope to illumine that answer even further by unpacking the kingdom message of the Gospels.

Our goal in this study is to understand what Jesus means by "the kingdom of God" (and related terms) and to contextualize it in the light of its Old Testament background. This will require us to use both a broad lens and a narrow lens: a broad lens to look at all of Scripture, and a narrow lens to focus on specific texts in the Gospels. We will look both at Christ's kingdom *teaching* and at His kingdom *work* in relation to our salvation. We will therefore also embark on this journey with an eye to practical living: Why does it matter? As we will see, the message of the kingdom is not ultimately different from the message of the gospel.

Following the Map: How to Read the Gospels

This is a book on the kingdom and the Gospels. To prepare for the journey of this study, we need to follow the proper map. Simply put, we need to interpret the Gospels in the right way. Yet if we look at the history of scholarship, we may find this easier said than done. What is the best way to read the Gospels? What is their genre? Why are there four of them? How should we read them for edification? A few words on these matters will help us gain our bearings for the rest of this journey.

Four Errors to Avoid

To understand the right way to read the Gospels, it will be helpful to consider some misguided approaches.

First, it is misguided to doubt the truth or historicity of the Gospels. We must read them not with an attitude of skepticism but with an attitude of trust. Maybe this sounds intuitive, but much scholarship on the Gospels (and the kingdom) does not share this perspective. Instead of being seen as four authoritative, infallible writings, the Gospels are often viewed as documents that reflect the fallible interpretations of early Christians. It is too often assumed that the accounts of the Gospels are not entirely trustworthy or historical. It is routinely said that where the gospel accounts differ, the writers responsible for those changes were inserting their own views into the text, perhaps even correcting the other Gospels. This view means that Jesus may not have said or done what the text says He said or did. It is thus assumed by many that some portions of the Gospels are historical (which portions the educated historian can ascertain), but other portions are manifestly nonhistorical.

But this approach is unsustainable. It is self-defeating; it pits the Gospels against one another, using them to disprove themselves. It also does not reflect the proper attitude toward the Gospels, which is to be one of submission and trust. These books are entirely trustworthy, including what they say about the kingdom.

Second, it is misguided to isolate the Gospels from each other. We must appreciate that in God's providence we have *four* authoritative Gospels. This means we must listen to all four. Too often, those who write about the Gospels consider each one in isolation from the others, and each one is read as though we have blinders to the others. This can lead to interpretations of individual passages that would not stand if the parallel passages were allowed to illumine the text.

Instead, we should read the Gospels as four distinct but unified books about Jesus. We should read each book considering the other three, gaining illumination from parallel passages. For example, in Mark, John the Baptist predicts that Jesus will baptize with the Holy Spirit (1:8), but in Matthew and Luke, John predicts that Jesus will baptize with the Holy Spirit and fire (Matt. 3:11; Luke 3:16). The addition of "and fire" clarifies what Mark's gospel means by the shorter version "Holy Spirit."

Third, it is misguided to flatten out the differences between the Gospels, as if they were all carbon copies of each other. This is the corollary to the previous danger: Just as we must not isolate any gospel from the other three, so we also must not fail to observe carefully the intentional wording and structure of any individual gospel. We need to read synthetically all four Gospels, but we also need to read each gospel carefully. Where the Gospels differ, we must ask why they differ. The answer is not because they are contradictory but because each gospel presents Jesus and His message in distinctive ways.

For example, in Mark, Jesus appears on the scene and is baptized by John with hardly any backstory. Matthew is different. His gospel begins with a genealogy, the virginal conception of Jesus, the story of Jesus' birth, and some episodes of His childhood before His baptism by John. Readers of Mark are presented with a fast-paced narrative that jumps right into the action with Jesus as an adult, whereas Matthew carefully explains Jesus' lineage and the scriptural conformity of His childhood before His public ministry. These are not contradictory but wonderfully complementary.

Fourth, it is misguided to pluck out smaller units of the Gospels and read them in isolation from the surrounding contexts. It makes a significant difference where a reader is within the narrative of a gospel when reading a particular passage in it.

This means that we need to resist the approach that reads the Gospels as though they were isolated maxims of philosophy that we can "cut and paste." Such an approach threatens to miss the proper context for reading the Gospels. Yes, they are to be read for personal edification, but they must also be read in their proper contexts. Think of reading the Gospels like being on a road trip where we take in all the sights along the way and contextualize each story within the larger framework. All the twists and turns should make more sense by the time we get to the end. This also means that we need to keep Jesus and His work front and center. This brings us to three positive landmarks to keep in view when we read the Gospels.

Three Helpful Landmarks

To understand what the kingdom means, we need to read the Gospels rightly. I have already alluded to some of the proper approaches in contrast to the wrong approaches. Here I give three positive landmarks to guide us on the way. In one sense, these all hinge on the same principle: We need to read the Gospels contextually. But what does that mean?

First, we need to read the Gospels considering their primary background: the Old Testament. This is clear from the frequency with which the Gospels quote from and allude to the Old Testament. If you're familiar with the Gospels, then this is probably not surprising. The gospel writers quite often draw attention to the Old Testament when they quote it. But how does this realization affect your interpretation of the Gospels? It should affect it a great deal. One helpful question to ask when you come to a difficult passage in the Gospels is, Does this idea have a background in the Old Testament? If it does, it is likely that attending to that background will help you understand the New Testament passage. I will illustrate this in detail in the following chapter, but it will apply to all the remaining chapters in some way.

Second, we need to read the Gospels considering their genre as *narratives*. The Gospels are not collections of religious maxims. Neither are the Gospels collections of sayings of Jesus; this was a mistaken view of some previous scholarship. To be sure, the Gospels contain many *sayings* of Jesus. But those sayings of Jesus must be understood in the context of the overall narrative of each gospel. Put in everyday terms, the Gospels are stories. They have a beginning, a middle, and an end. We need, therefore, to read them as stories, allowing the plot to develop, tensions to rise, and resolution to be found. This means that we will know more about the kingdom the further we read in the Gospels; what might be only vaguely understood in earlier chapters will probably gain greater clarity as we get closer to the end of the book.

If this sounds like a new way to read the Gospels, be encouraged that we already have a lot of practice with this. We are all familiar with stories. We tell them, read them, and watch them. If you watch a movie, you may not know at the beginning who the good guys and the bad guys really are. Sometimes you're surprised when you find out later. A situation that may seem to be unfolding one way at the beginning can turn out differently by the end. Further, you probably don't watch movies by skipping from the beginning to the end, back to the middle, back to the beginning, then to the end, and so on. We watch them sequentially from beginning to end, following the unfolding plot and character development.

These skills can help us when reading the Gospels; they are stories. We should develop the skill of reading them from beginning to end. What may not be clear at the beginning is clearer by the end. This is why readings that isolate passages from their contexts can be counterproductive. Something that occurs or is stated early in a gospel may not be the final insight on a topic but is part of a developing storyline. We will learn more if we keep reading. We therefore need to know where we are in the gospel to make sense of a particular passage.

An example may help. Scholars debate what Jesus means by "Son of Man." Many backgrounds have been suggested, but the best option is that it derives from "son of man" in Daniel 7:13–14. Yet this is not clear the first few times Jesus uses the title. It does, however, become clearer as the Gospels progress, as Jesus speaks more and more of the authority of the Son of Man. And at the end of the Gospels, when He is asked specifically about His sonship, Jesus quotes from Daniel 7:13 to explain who He is as Son of Man (see Mark 14:61–62). That later insight can then in turn help illumine earlier references to "Son of Man" that do not include quotations of Daniel 7. This Old Testament background given at the end of the gospel provides clarity for earlier portions and illumines the meaning of the kingdom, as we will see in later chapters.

Third, we must always read the Gospels with a focus on Christ, who is the protagonist. We must relate every story, every event to Jesus. This means that when we read about the kingdom, we must not read it in a way that abstracts the kingdom teaching from the person and work of Jesus. Jesus is the anointed King of the kingdom. This is one of the goals of the present study: to explain the meaning of the kingdom in relation to Jesus and what He does.

An illustration may give clarity. One of the texts about the kingdom that has often been misunderstood (and perhaps even mistranslated) is Luke 17:20–21. The English Standard Version reads:

> Being asked by the Pharisees when the kingdom of God would come, he answered them, "The kingdom of God is not coming in ways that can be observed, nor will they say, 'Look, here it is!' or 'There!' for behold, the kingdom of God is in the midst of you."

If you are familiar with other translations, you may notice that this last phrase "the kingdom of God is in the midst of you" has also been rendered in the King James Version as "the kingdom of God is within you." While this latter option is a possible translation, the context of Luke 17 makes it extremely unlikely. In Luke 17, Jesus confronts skeptical Pharisees who do not believe His message. To them Jesus is not giving a general truism that the kingdom of God is already inside them. That does not fit the context, and it also does not reflect the centrality of Christ in this saying.

Instead, the ESV is correct in its translation "in the midst of you." To understand what this means requires us to consider what was in their midst at that time—or better, *who* was in their midst. This is most likely a reference to Jesus, who was right in front of them, though they did not understand rightly. Jesus is central in this saying, for Jesus is central to the kingdom of God.

To read the Gospels rightly—and to understand the kingdom rightly—we need always to keep our eyes on Jesus.

A Bumpy Road

Luke 17:20–21 provides a helpful introduction to this next topic, for too often the kingdom of God has been misunderstood. One of the best ways to avoid misunderstanding the kingdom is to read statements about it in their proper contexts with the proper interpretive approach. I will illustrate three ways that the kingdom has been misunderstood before offering a preliminary definition to give us a running start into this study.

First, some have viewed the kingdom simply as a noble ideal or an ethical principle about how we live.[1] This approach could be combined with misguided optimism in the inherent goodness of humankind and humanity's aspirations to reach ever-higher planes of dignity and enlightenment. It reduces Jesus' teaching about the kingdom to our actions. If the point of the kingdom of God is what we do in response to Jesus' teaching, then the focus moves significantly away from Jesus and onto us. Where is the good news in that? What is the role of Jesus in bringing such a view to fruition? Where is the teaching about Jesus' overcoming sin? This approach does not reflect the biblical texts. It does not address the work of Christ sufficiently, nor does it address sufficiently the problem of our sin. It is also too decontextualized from the Old Testament concept of what the kingdom means.

---

1 For more on the various views of the kingdom, see Herman N. Ridderbos, *The Coming of the Kingdom*, trans. H. de Jongste, ed. Raymond O. Zorn (Presbyterian and Reformed, 1962), xii–xxxii.

Second, some have viewed the kingdom as a social movement that favors the poor over the rich. With this view, the kingdom overcomes the power structures of our present age, and God favors the poor and weak instead of the rich and powerful. This is associated with what is known as the social gospel and with liberation theology.[2] Doesn't Jesus refer to His ministry as good news for the poor in Luke 4:18? Yet despite the true affirmation that Jesus speaks of the kingdom as good news for the poor, viewing the kingdom as a social movement misses the transcendent elements of it; the kingdom is not something that we produce through our actions but is established through the work of Christ. Further, viewing the kingdom through the primary lens of a social movement does not sufficiently address the reality that our primary problem is not economic but moral. In other words, our primary problem is sin. Such viewpoints also fail to do justice to the biblical reality that a person's economic status does not guarantee favor with God; in Scripture it is possible for the rich to be favored and for the poor to be critiqued. The kingdom is not promised carte blanche to any specific economic demographic but is promised to those who love God (James 2:5). This social view of the kingdom fails for similar reasons as the first view.

Third, it has often been difficult to nail down exactly *when* the kingdom comes. Some have viewed the kingdom as entirely here

---

2 See Stephen J. Nichols, "The Kingdoms of God: The Kingdom in Historical and Contemporary Perspectives," in *The Kingdom of God*, ed. Christopher W. Morgan and Robert A. Peterson (Crossway, 2012), 26–29; see also the editors' introduction, 21–22.

already with no future consummation in view.[3] This view misses the importance of the return of Christ, which the Gospels relate to the future reality of the kingdom (see Matt. 19:28; Luke 22:28–30). Others view the kingdom as something that is entirely future.[4] This view does not adequately account for texts such as Luke 17:20–21 and similar texts that indicate that the kingdom is already present. Instead, it is now widely appreciated that the kingdom is both already present (beginning with the ministry of Jesus) and not yet fully perfected in this age. We will see this further as the book progresses.

Defining the Destination

So how should we understand the kingdom? Answering this question will take most of the rest of this book. This study will proceed inductively as we look at key passages in the Gospels, considering their near and far contexts with a particular focus on the nature of the kingdom in relation to Christ. Though this concept of the kingdom has been widely debated, with the right approach to the Gospels, we can think afresh about this important question and do our best to ensure that our answer is built on as wide a scriptural foundation as possible.

I am therefore not going to venture a detailed definition to this question at this point in the book. We need to work our way through the texts before coming to a fuller definition. But to warm us up, I offer here a memorable single-sentence definition, along with a bit

---

3 See R.T. France, "Kingdom of God," in *Dictionary for Theological Interpretation of the Bible*, ed. Kevin J. Vanhoozer (Baker Academic, 2005), 422, noting C.H. Dodd.

4 Ridderbos, *Coming of the Kingdom*, xii–xvi, noting especially J. Weiss and A. Schweitzer. See also France, "Kingdom of God," 422.

of explanation. This is not an exhaustive definition but one that will help kick-start our journey.

One of the great minds in biblical theology over the past couple hundred years was Geerhardus Vos (1862–1949). One of his works, which has influenced my own understanding of the kingdom, focuses on the kingdom of God.[5] In this short work, he sets out some basic parameters for what was expected when the kingdom would come: "The kingdom, it was believed, comes when the gospel is spread, hearts are changed, sin and error overcome, righteousness cultivated, a living communion with God established."[6] This definition is not the final word on the kingdom, but it will serve as a starting point for our study.

Notice a few aspects of this definition as we prepare for a further study of the kingdom. First, notice the close connection between the kingdom and the gospel. The kingdom message is the gospel message. These are not two different messages, and they both focus on Jesus Christ.

Second, notice that the kingdom entails heart change. The kingdom is not a social movement. It does not result in only external change. Since the kingdom message is the gospel message, the kingdom includes sinners turning from sin and to God in submission to Him, receiving forgiveness of sins.

Third, where the kingdom spreads, sin and error are overcome. The Gospels show us how Jesus came to destroy the works of the devil (1 John 3:8), ultimately through His death and resurrection.

---

5 Geerhardus Vos, *The Teaching of Jesus Concerning the Kingdom of God and the Church*, 2nd ed. (American Tract Society, 1903).

6 Vos, *Teaching of Jesus*, 39.

But sin and error are also overcome practically in God's people. This correlates to the cultivation of righteous living in fellowship with the true God of the whole world.

Fourth, I would add to Vos' definition that the phrase *kingdom of God* refers to the special rule of God in our world but not to the neglect of a place over which he rules.[7] The kingdom of God is therefore both a reign and a domain.

There is still more to say. We need to be sure that we recognize that something big is happening in the Gospels. The long-awaited expectations of the kingdom were beginning to come to fruition. This is another way of saying that the kingdom in the Gospels is *eschatological*—it deals with the great, future hopes of God's people when God would intervene powerfully and finally on behalf of His people.

This is the kingdom that Jesus teaches about that finds its roots in the Old Testament. Understanding the kingdom message of Jesus therefore requires us first to look back to the Old Testament. It is to that context we turn in the next chapter.

---

7 See also Ridderbos, *Coming of the Kingdom*, 24–25.

Practical Takeaways

1. Let us be thankful that we have four Gospels that collectively provide a more well-rounded picture of our Savior than any one gospel. Further, let us trust these Gospels and look at them intently to understand what they say about the kingdom and how this relates to Christ.
2. Part of the beauty of the Gospels is the way that they communicate Christ and His kingdom to us in the form of narratives. Develop the skill of reading the Gospels sequentially, with particular attention to the unfolding drama, the plot, the characters, and the resolution.
3. The kingdom message is closely related to the gospel message. We must keep this supernatural understanding of the kingdom before us throughout this study. And since the kingdom message is the gospel message, we may also find that the Gospels are rich resources for our understanding of the gospel message.

2

The Context for the Kingdom

Maybe you've had the experience of joining a conversation already underway and feeling lost. For you to understand what is going on, someone needs to catch you up. Or maybe you want to watch a ballgame on TV, but you turn it on halfway through. If so, you may wonder what the score is and how it came to be that way. We make sense of many things by the intuitive use of context. A punch in one context may be playful but in another context may start a fight. Context matters a great deal.

The same is true for our understanding of the kingdom of God. If we start with the New Testament as the foundation for what the kingdom means, we may find ourselves in the middle of a conversation that we don't fully understand. In the first century, the people of God shared some expectations about what the kingdom means that were assumed by Jesus—even as He challenged some of those expectations. In other words, Jesus was not the first to introduce the concept of the kingdom. Scripture has much to say about the kingdom in the Old Testament. What Jesus says about the kingdom must be slotted into that context and understood in the light of those expectations. It will take us a bit more work to recover what those expectations were, but recovering them will go far in helping us understand the nature of the kingdom in the New Testament.

While the Old Testament does not speak about the kingdom with the same frequency as the New Testament, it would be wrong to conclude that the concept is foreign to the Old Testament. The kingdom of God permeates the Old Testament.

In this chapter, I want to explore in more detail the Old Testament background to the kingdom—which is substantial. Kingdom expectations start early in the Old Testament, but they really come into their own with David and his kingdom. David was the paradigmatic king of God's kingdom in the Old Testament, and the Lord made a covenant with David that one of his sons would rule over the kingdom forever. Yet we also find great tragedy among God's people in the Old Testament, with the kingship and the kingdom falling to the enemies of God's people. Even so, God's promises remained. It is in the light of such promises that we should understand the kingdom in the New Testament and Jesus' identity as the messianic Son of David.

Foundations of the Kingdom

The Old Testament foundations of the kingdom of God are laid at the beginning in creation. Already God is portrayed as a great King whose power is apparent over creation. His resting on the seventh day of creation communicates that He has successfully completed His task of creation; He rests when His work of creation is completed.

The creation of humanity in God's image also reflects the divine kingship of God. Man and woman are created in God's image and commanded to rule over God's creation (Gen. 1:26–28). This ruling over creation is part of what it means to be made in the image of God: Adam and Eve were to be royal image bearers of the Great King and to spread His glory throughout the whole world.[1] The royal dignity of humanity, therefore, reflects God's divine kingship. This is reiterated later in the Psalms when David, reflecting on the creation in Genesis 1–2, speaks of the crowning with glory and honor that is characteristic of humanity (Ps. 8:5). If humanity, made in the image of God, is crowned with glory and honor, we can be sure that this is but a reflection of the kingship of God.

With the fall of humanity into sin in Genesis 3, the kingdom of God as it was in the beginning, as it was to be ruled over by Adam, was marred. Sin brought disorder and disruption and pain. God never ceased to be King, but now there is a conflict that will play out throughout Scripture and world history. It is a kingdom conflict between the offspring of the woman and the offspring of the serpent. This is the context for understanding the great gospel promise of Genesis 3:15, which foretells a coming Redeemer. Speaking to the serpent, whom He was cursing, the Lord God said,

> "I will put enmity between you and the woman,
>   and between your offspring and her offspring;
> he shall bruise your head,
>   and you shall bruise his heel."

---

1 See, e.g., Richard L. Pratt Jr., *Designed for Dignity: What God Has Made It Possible for You to Be*, 2nd ed. (P&R, 2000), 23–38; and G.K. Beale, *The Temple and the Church's Mission: A Biblical Theology of the Dwelling Place of God*, New Studies in Biblical Theology 17 (IVP, 2004), 81–87.

This promised Seed of the woman refers to a coming child who would destroy the devil and his kingdom and recover what Adam lost in the beginning.

God is portrayed in Scripture as a great King (see Ps. 10:16),[2] and those made in His image are also portrayed in royal terms. The same is true for Israel collectively. In the exodus from Egypt, Pharaoh is commanded to let Israel—the Lord's firstborn son—go, or Pharaoh's firstborn son would be killed (Ex. 4:22–23). This is a challenge of kingships. Pharaoh's royal son would die if he would not let the royal son of the Lord go free. The story of the exodus is therefore the vindication of the true kingship of the Lord. This perspective continues in Deuteronomy, where the Lord is identified as a great King—or Father—who cares for His people. This is a significant emphasis of Deuteronomy (see 1:31; 8:5; 14:1–2; 32:4–6, 18–20). The people collectively were God's son, which paved the way for one individual to lead the nation as God's son.

Deuteronomy 17:14–17 specifically anticipates a future day when God's people would be led by a king according to the instruction of the Lord:

> When you come to the land that the Lord your God is giving you, and you possess it and dwell in it and then say, "I will set a king over me, like all the nations that are around me," you may indeed set a king over you whom the Lord your God will choose. One from among your brothers you shall set as king over you. You may not put a foreigner over you, who is not your brother. Only he must not acquire many horses for himself or cause the people to

2 See also Ridderbos, *Coming of the Kingdom*, 4.

> return to Egypt in order to acquire many horses, since the LORD has said to you, "You shall never return that way again." And he shall not acquire many wives for himself, lest his heart turn away, nor shall he acquire for himself excessive silver and gold.

In the future, the Lord would choose a king for God's people who would rule them according to God's word, not according to the customs of the nations. This king, as we will see, would be God's Son and would rule over God's son (that is, God's people) collectively. This again reflects the divine royalty of God Himself, for the king of God's people rules on behalf of God, the Great King. Instead of trusting in chariots or horses, this king over God's people was to trust in the name of the Lord (see Ps. 20:7–9). He would lead the people in righteousness and protect God's people from their enemies, allowing them to serve and worship the Lord in the promised land. In the days of Deuteronomy, the people had no earthly king, but this would change in the future.

The book of Judges further underscores why God's people need a king. Judges recounts cycles of sin and rebellion and how the Lord raised up judges (or warlords) to save His people.[3] Yet the deliverance through the judges did not last, and by the end of the book, sin had gotten grossly out of hand. Judges makes clear that the people went their own way because they did not have a king. For example, just before recounting great corruption in Israel, the book of Judges states, "In those days there was no king in Israel" (18:1). A similar refrain

3 On this and the role of the judges, see Bruce K. Waltke with Charles Yu, *An Old Testament Theology: An Exegetical, Canonical, and Thematic Approach* (Zondervan, 2007), 588–623.

opens chapter 19, just before one of the great atrocities of the Old Testament. The book ends ominously: "In those days there was no king in Israel. Everyone did what was right in his own eyes" (21:25).

The implication of Judges is that God's people went astray in large measure because they had no king to rule over them in righteousness and provide safety from their enemies. The book of Judges therefore provides dramatic illustrations of why it is good and proper for God's people to be ruled over by God's king.

The Kingdom of David

The Davidic Covenant

In the days of the prophet Samuel, the people finally got their king. While it is true that Samuel rebuked the people for their reasons for wanting a king—to be like the other nations (1 Sam. 8:4–9)—the appropriateness of a king's ruling over God's people was already clear from books such as Deuteronomy and Judges. The first king was Saul, the son of Kish, who was an impressive physical specimen but had the fatal flaw of not trusting in the Lord. Therefore, the Lord rejected him as king, and David was anointed in his place.

David is the most important king in the Old Testament. He was a man after God's own heart (1 Sam. 13:14), and he was the paradigmatic king. Further, and crucial for understanding the kingdom in the New Testament, it was with David that the Lord made a covenant promising an everlasting kingdom. This is recounted in 2 Samuel 7:

> "Thus says the LORD of hosts, I took you from the pasture, from following the sheep, that you should be prince over my people Israel. And I have been with you wherever you went and have cut

> off all your enemies from before you. And I will make for you a great name, like the name of the great ones of the earth. And I will appoint a place for my people Israel and will plant them, so that they may dwell in their own place and be disturbed no more. And violent men shall afflict them no more, as formerly, from the time that I appointed judges over my people Israel. And I will give you rest from all your enemies. Moreover, the LORD declares to you that the LORD will make you a house. When your days are fulfilled and you lie down with your fathers, I will raise up your offspring after you, who shall come from your body, and I will establish his kingdom. He shall build a house for my name, and I will establish the throne of his kingdom forever. I will be to him a father, and he shall be to me a son. When he commits iniquity, I will discipline him with the rod of men, with the stripes of the sons of men, but my steadfast love will not depart from him, as I took it from Saul, whom I put away from before you. And your house and your kingdom shall be made sure forever before me. Your throne shall be established forever." (vv. 8–16)

This divine promise is known as the Davidic covenant. In this covenant, the Lord promises to build David a house—that is, a dynastic kingdom—for his offspring (2 Sam. 7:11–12). The kingdom of David's offspring would not be temporary but would last forever (vv. 13, 16). The king would be God's son, ruling over God's people as God's chosen representative (v. 14). While David ruled on God's behalf with great success, David's greater Son would rule over God's people forever. The Davidic kingdom would never end. The coming of this Davidic offspring (v. 12) fulfills the Abrahamic promise of an offspring from Abraham (Gen. 15:4) and ultimately fulfills the promise that the offspring of the woman would bruise the head of the devil (3:15).

David plays a key role in establishing the kingdom of God in the Old Testament. But the Davidic covenant looks beyond David to an even greater Son who would rule forever. David was a great king who ruled God's people well and protected them from their enemies. But he was also a deeply flawed man, and his kingdom tottered in the latter years of his reign.

David's son Solomon rose to even greater heights than David. Could Solomon perhaps be the promised son who would reign forever? It may have looked that way at first. But Solomon was not the final son to reign forever. Like David, Solomon, as great as he was, turned away from the Lord toward the end of his life (1 Kings 11). The Davidic covenant looked for further fulfillment beyond Solomon. A greater Son of David—greater than Solomon—would one day come and rule forever. It is in such light that the New Testament presents Jesus as greater than David (Matt. 12:1–8) and greater than Solomon (v. 42).

The Davidic Covenant in the Psalms

The Psalms have much to say about the Davidic covenant and this coming Son who would rule forever. He would be called God's Son and would one day rule over the nations (Ps. 2:7–9). This psalm sets much of the tone for the rest of the Psalter, which, to a significant degree, is focused on the king and his kingdom. Notice how often the Psalms depict the success of the king or the kingdom (some examples include Pss. 2; 20–21; 45; 72; 89; 110; 118; 132).

All of God's people can read the Psalms individually and collectively for great edification, and they do well to notice a common thread of hope that focuses our attention on the deliverance that comes from God's chosen king. When we read the Psalms, our attention should often be focused on God's Anointed who will deliver God's people. This king would be like David, but greater. This is the king to whom David looked forward and who would fulfill the Davidic covenant. This is why we can celebrate Psalm 45, which is a wedding feast for a king, because Jesus is the divine King who takes His people to Himself forever. This is why we can rejoice in Psalm 72:1 ("Give the king your justice, O God, and your righteousness to the royal son!"), for the One who rules over God's people does so in righteousness (v. 2), and His peace abounds forever (v. 7). This is good news not just for the king but for the people over whom he rules. Jesus is the ultimate fulfillment of this psalm.

Psalm 40 is another example where the royal focus helps us understand the psalm's relation to Christ. David writes of himself that he has come to do God's will as it is written of him in the book, and his delight is in God's law (vv. 7–8). The book that David has in view here may well be the laws for the king that we read about in Deuteronomy 17. David ruled in accord with these. Yet David himself was deeply flawed and struggled with his own sinfulness (see Ps. 40:12). But the letter to the Hebrews explains that Jesus' obedience fulfills Psalm 40 to a greater degree than David's obedience did, for Jesus' obedience was wedded to His final sacrifice bringing full atonement for sins (Heb. 10:5–10). Jesus is the greater David who was entirely committed to the will of God, and He reigns forever (Heb. 1:8, quoting Ps. 45:6).

Additionally, this coming King would be greater than David because He is not only David's son, but He is also David's

Lord (Ps. 110:1). This is an important text that we will return to in chapter 13. Such examples could be multiplied many times over.

The Davidic covenant, therefore, provides the backdrop for the theology of the kingdom in the Psalms and shows the close relationship between *covenant* and *kingdom*. The Davidic covenant would be fulfilled when the greater Son of David arrived to reign over God's people.

The Kingdom Structure of the Psalms

The importance of the Davidic covenant in the Psalms shows us that the kingdom of God is central. The first two psalms introduce the entire book, and Psalm 2 focuses explicitly on the kingship of the royal Son of David, and understanding this informs how we read the entire book of Psalms. In other words, we need to read the Psalms with an awareness of how they speak of the king of Israel.[4]

Further, the Psalms are divided into five books, and scholars often relate the topical content of these books to the various stages of the kingdom. These books have been given various titles by scholars, but they often focus on the kingship or the kingdom. The following represents one way of describing the contents of the five books:[5]

---

4 Ian J. Vaillancourt, *Treasuring the Psalms: How to Read the Songs That Shape the Soul of the Church* (IVP Academic, 2023), 42–58; and Bruce K. Waltke and Fred G. Zaspel, *How to Read and Understand the Psalms* (Crossway, 2023), 73–81.

5 These come from Vaillancourt, *Treasuring the Psalms*, 60–77; see also O. Palmer Robertson, *The Flow of the Psalms: Discovering Their Structure and Theology* (P&R, 2019), 50–52; Mark D. Futato, *Interpreting the Psalms: An Exegetical Handbook*, Handbooks for Old Testament Exegesis (Kregel, 2007), 80–81; and Waltke and Zaspel, *How to Read*, 477–97.

Books 1–2 (Pss. 1–72): the tears of David as he reigns in tension
Book 3 (Pss. 73–89): the exile and loss of kingship
Book 4 (Pss. 90–106): the Lord reigns even when David does not
Book 5 (Pss. 107–50): the return of a new and better David

This Davidic orientation in Psalm 2 to the entire Psalter and the overall kingdom structure of the Psalter show us how central the kingdom is in the Psalms. The Davidic covenant provides the context for understanding much of what we read about in the Psalms. The kingdom flows from the Davidic covenant, for in that covenant the Lord promises an everlasting kingdom. Since the Psalms are so frequently referenced in the Gospels and are central to them, we do well to take account of how important the kingdom is in the Psalms, which is a book about God's king and God's kingdom. They provide crucial background for understanding what Jesus means by the kingdom.

The Failure of the Kingdom

While the kingdom of God is on display in the Davidic covenant and in the Psalms, the historical books of the Old Testament broadly are all about the successes and struggles of various stages of God's kingdom. In the words of theologian Herman Bavinck, "What Scripture describes in these books . . . is the progress of the kingdom of God."[6]

This history in the remainder of the Old Testament is filled with ups and downs—many downs. After the heights of Solomon's

6 Herman Bavinck, *The Wonderful Works of God: Instruction in the Christian Religion According to the Reformed Confession*, trans. Henry Zylstra (Westminster Seminary Press, 2019), 74.

glorious reign, the kingdom split under his son Rehoboam into the Southern Kingdom of Judah and the Northern Kingdom of Israel. The account of these events and the ensuing years is recorded in 1–2 Kings and 1–2 Chronicles. In the north, idolatry was established early on by Jeroboam, who built a rival place of worship to Jerusalem. We read of a succession of ungodly kings in the north, such as Ahab (and his wife, Jezebel). Ahab worshiped Baal, murdered Naboth, and stole his vineyard, and during his reign the prophets were killed (see 1 Kings 16–22). Such failures of ungodly kingship led to a failure of the kingdom, with the Northern Kingdom eventually falling to the Assyrians in 722 BC.

In the Southern Kingdom things were not quite as bad, but they were bad enough. Some kings, such as Hezekiah, carried David's mantle admirably (if imperfectly). But the overall trajectory even of the Southern Kingdom was not success but failure. The Southern Kingdom lasted longer, but it, too, fell to foreign enemies, succumbing to the Babylonians by 586 BC.

With the fall of the kingdom and kingship, the people languished. Many were taken into exile and forced into foreign lands. Idolatry ran rampant. The temple at Jerusalem was devastated. There was little peace for God's people. The lament of Psalm 137 reflects the despondency of God's people in the absence of their king:

> By the waters of Babylon,
> there we sat down and wept,
> when we remembered Zion. (v. 1)

But the promise of the Davidic covenant was a guarantee that the kingdom would not be permanently cut off.

The Promise of a Restored Kingdom

Thankfully, the failure of the kingdom was not the final word. Even when it might have looked to the naked eye as if the kingdom of God had been shattered beyond repair, the promise of an everlasting kingdom from David's line was never in doubt—for God had promised. And God's promises are certain.

The Old Testament prophets often recalled this Davidic covenant in their prophecies of the future restoration of God's kingdom. This is prominent in Isaiah. Indeed, Isaiah 9:2–7, a familiar Christmas passage, is not just about a child to be born—as wonderful as that is—but about a *royal* child to be born, the coming Son of David:

> The people who walked in darkness
> have seen a great light;
> those who dwelt in a land of deep darkness,
> on them has light shone.
> You have multiplied the nation;
> you have increased its joy;
> they rejoice before you
> as with joy at the harvest,
> as they are glad when they divide the spoil.
> For the yoke of his burden,
> and the staff for his shoulder,
> the rod of his oppressor,
> you have broken as on the day of Midian.
> For every boot of the tramping warrior in battle tumult
> and every garment rolled in blood
> will be burned as fuel for the fire.

> For to us a child is born,
> to us a son is given;
> and the government shall be upon his shoulder,
> and his name shall be called
> Wonderful Counselor, Mighty God,
> Everlasting Father, Prince of Peace.
> Of the increase of his government and of peace
> there will be no end,
> on the throne of David and over his kingdom,
> to establish it and to uphold it
> with justice and with righteousness
> from this time forth and forevermore.
> The zeal of the LORD of hosts will do this.

The people dwelling in darkness are those suffering the failure of their king and the violent threat of surrounding kingdoms. These are God's people, who faced the lowest of lows in their forced exile when the kingdom seemed to have disappeared. But in the face of such gloom would come a child to fulfill the Davidic covenant. This child would reign forever; of the increase of His kingdom and of peace there will be no end. As great as David's rule was, he did not fulfill this prophecy. His dynasty had fallen, but in the future, One would come to restore the fallen dynasty of David (Amos 9:11–12).

These are but a small sampling of the Old Testament expectations of the final fulfillment of the Davidic covenant. We will consider more Old Testament passages in the chapters that follow. These prophecies of a coming king remained unfulfilled in the Old Testament. But they come into spectacular view in the New Testament. It is to this story of the kingdom in the New Testament that we now turn our attention.

Practical Takeaways

1. God is the great King who reigns over the world. No one rivals His authority. We can be thankful that He is in control now and has always been in control.
2. As those made in the image of God, we are all called, as royal image bearers, to take the knowledge of God throughout the world. We are to "be fruitful and multiply" and reflect God's image throughout creation.
3. God's covenant promises will never be broken. He has promised that a Son of David would reign over the kingdom forever, and that is what we can celebrate with the coming of Christ.
4. The Psalms are not just prayers about us, but they are prayers in which we take refuge and solace in the promises of God about the kingdom and in the King. Let us take refuge in the King of Israel (Ps. 2:12).

3

The True King Arrives

"To be continued . . ." Don't you groan when you see these words at the end of a riveting show or movie? We want to see the story resolved and know what happens at the end. Does everything turn out? Do the good guys win? Does everyone live happily ever after? On the small screen, we may have to wait a week or a summer before finding out what happened. On the silver screen, it may take a year or more. We can't leave it at "to be continued." We need to know the end of the story.

Despite the proximity between the Old and New Testaments in our Bibles, the New Testament does not follow right after the events of the Old Testament. The Old Testament ends with something like "to be continued . . ."

In other words, God had promised His people a lasting kingdom and a king to reign forever. Despite the grand successes of God's people and kingdom under David and some of his descendants, the Old Testament does not end with the final resolution of the problems that God's people faced. Though God's people returned from exile and rebuilt the temple and the gates of Jerusalem, their experience paled in comparison to the fullness of blessings that would accrue to them when the Davidic kingdom was fully restored. They were still waiting.

The "to be continued" ending of the Old Testament looks ahead to the day when the kingdom of God would be reestablished and a king would be back on the throne. This king would overcome the problems evident among God's Old Testament people. This coming king would lead the people in righteousness. He would unify the fractured people of God. He would overcome opposition to God's people and grant them security in the promised land. The people would be free to worship the true God rightly.

In this chapter, I give much more attention to the kingdom in the Gospels of the New Testament. The gospel writers help us understand that Jesus of Nazareth is the promised Son of David, and His actions as King benefit His people. But before we turn there, we need to understand a bit more about the Old Testament expectations for the kingdom of God.

The Kingdom to Crush All Other Kingdoms

Nebuchadnezzar's Dream

We saw at the end of the previous chapter that God's people faced some trying times and were still anticipating the final Son of David who would crush all their opponents. In this section, we will consider another important Old Testament passage about the future kingdom and how it relates to other rivals to the kingdom of God.

The book of Daniel has much to say about the future kingdom of God and how it relates to other kingdoms. Later in this book,

I will explain how Jesus fulfills the vision of the Son of Man from Daniel 7 and how this relates to His kingdom. In what follows, I want us to consider what Daniel has to say about rival kingdoms to God's kingdom.

In Daniel 2, the Babylonian king Nebuchadnezzar had a troubling dream about a human statue composed of various materials. It had a head of gold, a chest and arms of silver, a midsection and thighs of bronze, legs of iron, and feet of iron and clay. As Daniel made clear to the king, these various materials and sections of the statue represented different kingdoms. Babylon was the head of gold; the silver most likely represented the Medo-Persians; the bronze, Greece; and the iron and clay, Rome. This iron kingdom would crush its opponents. This was a distressing image for God's people, who had no king on the throne.

Nebuchadnezzar's dream can be correlated to the rise and fall of competing kingdoms in the ancient Near East from the time of the Old Testament into the years of the so-called intertestamental period (between the ending of the Old Testament and the beginning of the New Testament).

But there is something else in this vision, something not part of the statue itself. Nebuchadnezzar also saw a stone uncut by human hands that crushed all the other kingdoms. Daniel explained the dream:

> "And in the days of those kings the God of heaven will set up a kingdom that shall never be destroyed, nor shall the kingdom be left to another people. It shall break in pieces all these kingdoms and bring them to an end, and it shall stand forever." (Dan. 2:44)

Daniel is referring to the kingdom of God, which would be established during the years of the kingdom of iron and clay (i.e., Rome). This is the kingdom that we read about in the New Testament. It starts in the humblest of ways but ends up outlasting the most powerful kingdom in the world, for the kingdom of God is established by the God of heaven.

Kingdoms That Did Not Last

The kingdoms of Nebuchadnezzar's statue were fierce and stood opposed to God and His people. But they did not last. They were not kingdoms that would stand forever. Though it may have seemed like they were unstoppable, they were all overcome within a few years. This was no surprise to God, and it is clear in Scripture. Indeed, all the kingdoms below (except Assyria) are foreseen in detail in the book of Daniel. Despite the power of these kingdoms, none of them would ultimately prevail against the kingdom of God.

Assyria. One of the kingdoms that did not last was the Assyrian Empire. This kingdom was not even represented on the statue in Nebuchadnezzar's dream because it had already been conquered by the Babylonians. Yet when you read the Old Testament and other ancient Near Eastern literature, you find that the Assyrians were an impressively intense and successful people. Their brutality was well known in the ancient world. It was to the Assyrians that the Northern Kingdom of Israel fell (see 2 Kings 17) in 722 BC. Later, the Assyrians threatened Jerusalem but were turned back by God's intervention (2 Kings 18–19). The Assyrians may have looked unstoppable, but Nahum prophesied that Assyria's capital, Nineveh, would be judged, and their kingdom was defeated by Babylon in 612 BC, around a hundred years after Assyria defeated Israel.

Babylon. Nebuchadnezzar was king of Babylon, which was represented by the head of gold in the statue he saw, and it was to the Babylonians and Nebuchadnezzar that the Southern Kingdom of Judah fell by 587/586 BC (see 2 Kings 25). This coincided with the ministry of Jeremiah, who warned God's people that the Babylonians were going to come and not to resist them, for they were God's instrument to discipline His people for their sin (see Jer. 27). Yet this did not mean that Babylon would escape God's judgment, for Jeremiah prophesied that Babylon would also fall (Jer. 50–51). The book of Daniel recounts how the kingdom indeed fell in the middle of the night to the Medo-Persians in 539/538 BC (Dan. 5:30–31). This was made clear to Daniel before it happened (vv. 18–30).

Medo-Persia. The book of Daniel recounts how the Babylonians fell to the Medes and the Persians, with the Mede Darius overtaking the Babylonian king Belshazzar (Dan. 5:28–31). Darius is perhaps the same king known elsewhere as Cyrus, whom the Lord used to bring His people back from captivity (Ezra 1–2; Isa. 45:1). Yet the Medo-Persians were not the final kingdom either. This kingdom oppressed God's people, but during the time of Queen Esther, the Lord providentially intervened to rescue His people during the reign of Ahasuerus (more commonly known as Xerxes). Yet as powerful as the Medo-Persian Empire was, it eventually fell to the Greeks and Alexander the Great in 334 BC. The fall of the Medo-Persian Empire was also foreseen by Daniel (Dan. 8:3–7, 20; 11:2).

Greece. Alexander the Great's empire stretched far and wide—but not as far as the kingdom of God stretches today. He conquered the Medo-Persians and extended his rule into much of the ancient world, from Europe, through North Africa, through ancient Palestine, and east to India. But his success was short-lived. His sprawling kingdom did not hold up, and Alexander died in 323 BC. His kingdom fractured into four segments marked by turmoil, infighting, and difficulty for God's people. These events were also prophesied by Daniel (Dan. 7:6; 8:7–14, 22–25; 11:5–35).

Rome. After the fall of the Greek Empire, the Jews retook control of the promised land for a while after the Maccabean revolt (167–164 BC), but they were unable to establish lasting independence or see the fulfillment of the Davidic covenant. The Romans marched into Jerusalem and captured it (and the temple) under Pompey the Great in 63 BC. This was the kingdom of clay and iron, more powerful than previous kingdoms, that Nebuchadnezzar saw in his dream about a statue. So powerful was Rome that it appeared that no one could stop this highly efficient and organized military juggernaut. Yet it was revealed to Daniel that this kingdom would not last forever. It would be crushed by the kingdom of God (Dan. 2:44; also 7:11–12), which is the kingdom of the Son of Man (7:13–14).

The coming kingdom of the Son of Man. In retrospect, none of the kingdoms from Nebuchadnezzar's statue lasted very long. They were all overcome by another kingdom in accord with God's sovereign rule over history. God knew the end from the beginning; all the kings and nations are to Him a drop in a bucket. Daniel recognized that God "removes kings and sets up kings" (2:21). And Nebuchadnezzar came to confess the true God:

> His dominion is an everlasting dominion,
>   and his kingdom endures from generation to generation;
> all the inhabitants of the earth are accounted as nothing,
>   and he does according to his will among the host of heaven
>   and among the inhabitants of the earth;
> and none can stay his hand
>   or say to him, "What have you done?" (4:34–35)

Nebuchadnezzar's realizations are consistent with Daniel's kingdom outlook, which encourages God's people that no kingdom arrayed against them will last forever and God is ultimately in charge of world history. His people will not be utterly cast off.

God's coming kingdom would be a work of God Himself. God must intervene to bring His kingdom in His time. The ungodly kingdoms that were not led by the light of God's law may have been powerful for a season; they may have looked unstoppable. But only God's kingdom lasts forever.

As the Old Testament concludes, the people are still waiting for their king and kingdom to arrive. The faithful were holding fast to the promises of a child from the line of David who would rule over God's kingdom forever. They were longing for the true King to arrive. The Gospels show us how God fulfilled these kingdom expectations.

The Long-Awaited King Is Born

In the years leading up to the New Testament, God's people longed for their true king to come and deliver them from the hand of their oppressors. They had the promises of a king who would reign over the kingdom of God forever, but none of the offspring of David had ever proved to be the final fulfillment of what was promised. But we find that final fulfillment in Jesus of Nazareth. He is the promised Son of David who reigns over the everlasting kingdom of God.

God's kingdom comes in God's time and in God's way, and we see this dramatically underscored in the way that this promised King was born, beginning on the first page of the New Testament. The Gospel of Matthew opens by identifying Jesus as "the son of David, the son of Abraham" (1:1), and then launches into an extended genealogy (vv. 2–17). Contemporary readers often do not find such genealogies as riveting as the first audience probably did. Reading biblical genealogies today might seem as interesting as reading a phone book or studying someone else's family tree. But Matthew shows us by this genealogy that Jesus is the true Son of David. He tells us of this King's supernatural birth. All this is good news for us. How so?

The first thing to observe is that the genealogy is focused on the kingship of Israel. This is not the genealogy of an isolated individual. This is a kingdom genealogy tracing the lineage of the true King of Israel. Jesus is the true Son of David and the true Israelite who represents His people collectively; He is the true Son of Abraham. Matthew's genealogy not only traces the lineage of Jesus but also summarizes the history of God's people through a kingdom lens. The genealogy explicitly mentions the deportation (or exile) to Babylon (Matt. 1:11–12) and then looks to the restoration beyond the exile (vv. 12–16). By summarizing the genealogy and focusing it on King David (v. 17), Matthew helps us see that the story of Jesus' lineage is the story of the continuing promise of God's kingdom.

This last point is entailed in Matthew 1:16: Jesus was born of Mary, and He is the Christ. The term *Christ* has become familiar, but we should not pass by it without realizing what it means. *Christ* is the Greek translation of the Hebrew term *messiah*. Put simply, the Christ is the Messiah. This refers to the anointed King who would rule forever. So Matthew's genealogy tells us that Jesus is the Son of David (v. 1), who is the promised Messiah to reign on David's throne.

But buried in this genealogy is something else remarkable: Jesus is born *of Mary* (v. 16). In contrast to the cadence of the genealogy, which speaks of the fatherly role of each previous generation, Jesus is born of Mary. This is an allusion to the virginal birth (or more technically, virginal conception) of Jesus. Jesus' birth was supernatural. It was not a result of the normal process of procreation. His birth marked divine intervention of the most glorious nature: the eternal Son of God being born of a woman, taking a true body and a reasonable soul to redeem His people. This virginal conception was fitting for One who is eternally the Son of God; in the incarnation the Son of God takes on human nature without ceasing to be the divine Son of God.

Jesus' birth may have been surprising, but it accorded with the prophecy spoken by Isaiah to King Ahaz that the virgin would conceive and bear a son (Isa. 7:14; Matt. 1:22–23). This word came amid kingdom conflict: King Ahaz of Judah was afraid of the kingdoms that were arrayed against him. Ahaz did not trust the word of the Lord enough to ask for a sign, but the Lord sent him a sign anyway. The kingdoms arrayed against Ahaz would not succeed (Isa. 7:7–9). The child to be born was Immanuel ("God with us"), the visible sign of God's presence with His people (v. 14). Though it seems that this prophecy was in one sense fulfilled in Isaiah's day, Jesus fulfills it in a greater way: He is truly God with us as the eternal Son of God, and His birth marks the coming of the kingdom that would outlast all other kingdoms.

The Gospel of Luke also highlights the royal, Davidic contours of Jesus' birth. When the angel Gabriel announces to Mary that she will have a son, he explains that this will be no ordinary child; this child is the heir to the Davidic throne:

> "And behold, you will conceive in your womb and bear a son, and you shall call his name Jesus. He will be great and will be called the Son of the Most High. And the Lord God will give to him the throne of his father David, and he will reign over the house of Jacob forever, and of his kingdom there will be no end." (Luke 1:31–33)

Mary was not just going to bear a child without having ever known a man; she was to give birth to the long-awaited Son of David, who would rule over God's kingdom forever. It is highly significant that Jesus' mother was a virgin. Since Jesus was not born through the ordinary means of procreation, He was not represented by Adam, who sinned. Jesus comes as the new Adam who is the Seed of the woman, fulfilling the promise of Genesis 3:15. Jesus is the One to bruise the head of the devil and overcome his kingdom, as the Gospels will explain elsewhere.[1]

This kingdom would come by means of God's appointed King. But for that kingdom to come, it would have to overcome opposing kingdoms. Many people had an idea of what this would look like, but the kingdom in the Gospels comes in a way they did not expect.

---

1 See further the discussions in chapters 4 and 7.

The Promised King Is Protected

It does not take long for the conflict to begin. In the opening chapters of Matthew, we meet King Herod the Great, who was ruling in Jerusalem. It seems, then, that God's people already had their king. But King Herod was not the true king. He was not the promised Son of David. In fact, his actions align more with Pharaoh of the exodus than with the God of Israel. King Herod did not have a genealogy that could be traced back to David. Herod was an Idumean. Idumea was an area south of Jerusalem and Judea, and Herod's lineage did not reflect the royal Davidic lineage.

How, then, was Herod a king? He was not the legitimate king of Israel. He did not rule by righteousness but with an iron fist. Nor was he a man who sought to purify the worship of Israel, for he built pagan idols. That Herod was able to stay in power for more than thirty years during Roman rule indicates his abilities as a flexible statesman. He ingratiated himself to his Roman overlords enough to be given some measure of independence, but he was not actually seeking first the kingdom of God and His righteousness. He was a squatter king whose grandiosity would soon come to an end after the birth of the true King.

It is significant that Jesus was born in Bethlehem, the city of David. This was a fitting birthplace for the true Son of David and fulfilled Scripture. Micah 5:2 predicted that the future Shepherd of Israel would come forth from Bethlehem. When the magi came from the east to worship the One who had been born King of the Jews, following the star they had seen, they naturally went to Jerusalem to find Him. But Jesus was not there. He was born in Bethlehem in accord with the prophecy of Micah. When the magi found Him in

Bethlehem, they brought Him royal gifts fit for a king: gold, frankincense, and myrrh. These magi's coming to worship from afar is one way we see that Jesus is a King for all the nations (see Isa. 60:1–3).

Herod was out to destroy Jesus—the threat to his throne. But God was in control. The wise men were warned in a dream not to return to Herod, and Joseph was warned in a dream to flee to Egypt. The Lord was not surprised at Herod's wicked schemes; He knew of them in advance, and He was orchestrating His plan of redemption to protect the chosen King.

When Herod realized that he had been foiled by the wise men, he decided to make sure Jesus was gone by wiping out all the male children in Bethlehem. He would be sure that no ruler would come out of Bethlehem to challenge his throne. But again, Herod failed. Jesus had already escaped to Egypt. In a dramatically ironic turn, Jesus had fled to Egypt to be protected from the purported king of Israel, but in this case it was Herod—*the king of Israel*—who took the lives of the Israelite children. This was not a king who was ruling in righteousness. Herod's actions were like Pharaoh's, the murderous actions of the seed of the serpent.

Jesus is not only the promised Son of David; He is also the Seed of the woman who is going to overcome the kingdom of the serpent. This reflects the meaning of His name, which is Jesus, "for he will save his people from their sins" (Matt. 1:21). The conflict continues from this point throughout the Gospels. But Jesus will overcome all opposition, establishing the kingdom of God and saving His people from their sins. These concepts of the kingdom and forgiveness are very much related, as I will argue in the next chapter.

Practical Takeaways

1. God knows the future and is working out His plan. Daniel was able to prophesy about the future rise and fall of kingdoms because God, who rules world history, made it known to him. The future is a mystery to us, but it is not a mystery to God. He is the One who makes mysteries known.
2. All earthly kingdoms will eventually fall, but Jesus' kingdom reigns forever. His kingdom is represented by the stone that crushes the statue of kingdoms in Nebuchadnezzar's dream. Jesus is the promised Son of David, and we should give Him our highest loyalty. Our hope is in Him and in His kingdom.
3. The Son of David is also the Son of God. He is the second person of the Trinity who came to save us from our sins, not because He was obligated to but because He loves us. He has come to destroy the serpent and deliver to us eternal life. This is what we read about in the Gospels.

4

The Gospel of the Kingdom

I don't know a lot about plumbing, but I have learned that a problem in one pipe may manifest itself in another location. I've encountered water not draining from a shower drain that had to be resolved by clearing the pipes in another area. Though they may seem like different issues, behind the scenes the pipes were connected.

That's often the way it is in life. Things that appear to be separate issues may be more closely related than we realize. Something similar can be said of the kingdom of God and the message of the gospel. Though these may seem like different topics, they're closely related.

In this chapter, I will say more about how the gospel is related to the kingdom of God. To understand the gospel rightly means that we must understand the kingdom rightly; Jesus preaches the gospel of the kingdom (Matt. 4:23; 9:35; 24:14).

If it is true that the kingdom constitutes the gospel message, then it is crucial to understand the kingdom if we want to get the gospel right. This also means that the kingdom message of the Gospels is good news (the meaning of *gospel*) for us. In this chapter, we will look at how the gospel is related to the kingdom and how the kingdom message of Jesus relates to His obedience on our behalf. The Gospels narrate how Jesus saves His people from their sins (Matt. 1:21) not only through His death and resurrection but also more comprehensively throughout His ministry.

In this chapter, I'll explain how the gospel rounds out our understanding of the kingdom and how the kingdom rounds out our understanding of the gospel.

The King Is Anointed

Jesus' baptism by John the Baptist marks the beginning of His kingdom ministry. Understanding what the baptism means helps us understand the good news of the kingdom message.

John's baptism was "a baptism of repentance for the forgiveness of sins" (Mark 1:4). John was a true prophet of God, calling God's people to turn from their wickedness and seek after true repentance, for a new work of God was imminent. The Lord was coming to redeem His people, and John was the voice in the wilderness preparing that way by preaching repentance (vv. 2–3). The people came to John confessing their sins (v. 5), but John also told the people that his ministry was not the main event; he was only the prelude to a bigger work. John pointed ahead to a Stronger One whose sandals he was not worthy to untie and who would baptize with the Holy Spirit and fire (Matt. 3:11; Mark 1:7–8).

John baptized with water, pointing to the need for God to wash the people's sins away. Responding positively to John's message meant responding positively to God's true prophet and recognizing the need for cleansing from sin. To heed John's message rightly also meant looking forward to the Stronger One, who would baptize in an even greater way than John. The Stronger One is Jesus, who came to John to be baptized. As we will see in the next chapter, Jesus' identity as the Stronger One correlates to His kingdom work, for it is as the Stronger One that He defeats the devil and frees His people from sin (see Mark 3:22–30).

Jesus responded positively to John's message and came to John to be baptized. But why was Jesus baptized if He was not a sinner? John the Baptist seemed to ask this question, for he would have hindered Jesus from being baptized, since he recognized Jesus' superiority (Matt. 3:14). Jesus' response is telling: "Let it be so now, for thus it is fitting for us to fulfill all righteousness" (v. 15). This is a cryptic statement, but it is apparent that Jesus' baptism by John is necessary. "To fulfill all righteousness" refers at some level to Jesus' work of redemption, and this work correlates to God's righteous requirements.

How, then, does the baptism contribute to Jesus' fulfillment of all righteousness?[1] Jesus is obeying the voice of God's prophet in solidarity with His people. Jesus does not have any need to confess His sins, but He submits to baptism as a way of identifying with those He came to save. Jesus' identification with His people points to His *representation* of His people. John's water baptism was a sign that indicated the need for God's people to be truly cleansed from sin, and that true cleansing John anticipated comes through the work of Jesus. Jesus' identification with His people's estate of sin points to the final cleansing provided by Jesus.

---

1 Jesus says it is fitting "for us" to fulfill all righteousness, including John in that work. John had an important work in the history of salvation, but the focus is on Jesus, as what follows in the Gospels makes clear.

Additionally, Jesus' baptism marks the beginning of His public ministry and His anointing for that work as the Messiah. Put another way, the baptism marks the anointing of King Jesus for His kingdom ministry. Notice what happens after Jesus is baptized: "And when he came up out of the water, immediately he saw the heavens being torn open and the Spirit descending on him like a dove. And a voice came from heaven, 'You are my beloved Son; with you I am well pleased'" (Mark 1:10–11).

The Spirit's descent on Jesus, seen in the form of a dove, does not mark the first filling of Jesus with the Holy Spirit. He was full of the Holy Spirit throughout His life. Instead, this marks the special anointing of Jesus for His messianic ministry (see Isa. 11:1–5). Remember that *messiah*, or *Christ*, means "anointed." Jesus' anointing was not just with water at His baptism but with the Holy Spirit. This anointing marked Jesus out as the King of the kingdom, and the Spirit empowered Jesus in His ministry. Peter would later explain in the book of Acts "how God anointed Jesus of Nazareth with the Holy Spirit and with power. He went about doing good and healing all who were oppressed by the devil, for God was with him" (10:38). As the Anointed One, Jesus is our Prophet, Priest, and King; all three of these were anointed offices in the Old Testament. We will see later in this study how Jesus is Prophet, Priest, and King, but the emphasis in the baptism is mostly on Jesus' kingship.

The kingship of Jesus is communicated especially by the fatherly voice that declares to Jesus, "You are my beloved Son." This is Old Testament language for the king, coming from Psalm 2:7. As I discussed in chapter 2, the Psalms largely focus on the coming royal Son of David. The heavenly voice at Jesus' baptism identifies Jesus as that long-awaited Son—the One who would rule finally and forever over God's kingdom. Jesus is both the eternal Son who has always existed and, as we saw from Matthew's genealogy, the long-awaited King who comes as David's son in fulfillment of the Davidic covenant. This is another way that we see Jesus' representation of His people: The king represents the people of God, and as the true King, Jesus represents His people. What He does benefits His people.

The voice from heaven, the voice of God the Father, also identifies Jesus as the Servant of Isaiah in the second part of His message: "With you I am well pleased" (Mark 1:11). This comes from Isaiah 42:1, which is the first of the four Servant Songs of Isaiah (42:1–9; 49:1–6; 50:4–9; 52:13–53:11). As the King, Jesus at the same time fulfills Isaiah's vision of the Servant whose message and work will benefit His people, seen most dramatically in His suffering on His people's behalf (note Isa. 53:4 in Matt. 8:17; Isa. 53:12 in Luke 22:37; see also Isa. 42:1–3 in Matt. 12:17–21).

Therefore, in His baptism Jesus identifies with His people and is proclaimed to be the true Son of David. As the true King, Jesus is the representative of His people. Jesus' actions, therefore, benefit those with whom He is in solidarity. Herein lies much of the rationale for why the kingdom is good news: Jesus is the King whose actions benefit those who look to Him in faith.

The King Obeys

The King Overcomes the Devil

Immediately after Jesus is baptized and anointed as the true King over God's people, He is led by the Spirit into the wilderness to be tempted by the devil (Matt. 4:1–11; Mark 1:12–13; Luke 4:1–13).

Despite the three temptations hurled by the devil, Jesus remains steadfast, trusting in the Word of God, and does not seek to alleviate His suffering or shortcut His calling. This is an event that has more to do with the kingdom than may seem at first glance.

How do you understand the significance of Jesus' temptation? His temptation has often been understood to be instructional for us—just as Jesus responded to the devil's temptations by three times quoting Scripture, so we also should rely on Scripture as we resist temptation. This is indeed good and right. But there is something more going on here than just Christ's serving as a model for us. His obedience in the face of temptation is the obedience of the King who has identified with His people, and His victory in the face of temptation directly benefits His people, who follow Him as King.

An analogy from the well-known Old Testament story of David and Goliath may help us understand. When David fought and defeated Goliath, he did not fight him simply as an isolated individual. This is where reading 1 Samuel sequentially (as we need to read the Gospels sequentially) is illuminating. Before David fought Goliath (1 Sam. 17), he had been anointed by Samuel as the king over Israel (ch. 16). The battle that David fought was, therefore, the battle of God's anointed king to save God's people. In this, David's valor contrasts with King Saul's reluctance to fight. David was a better king than Saul.

Similarly, in the Gospels Jesus is first anointed in His baptism before He overcomes the devil in the temptation accounts. Jesus' obedient victory also benefits His people; just as David's defeat of Goliath, the Philistines, and other enemies was good news for his people, who benefited from the king's actions, so Jesus' royal victory over the devil is good news for His people. Satan does not outsmart or trap Jesus. Instead, Jesus obeys truly, and the devil flees from Him (Matt. 4:10–11; Luke 4:13).

It is therefore important that we read the gospel accounts as sequential, unfolding narratives; it is only *after* Jesus is anointed for His public ministry that He faces the devil's temptations. These are, therefore, the temptations directed toward the representative of God's people, and the victory Jesus wins in the temptation is the victory He wins on behalf of His people.

This means that Jesus' obedience in the temptation is not just a model for how we should respond to temptation (though it does instruct us in that). Instead, the obedience of Jesus in the temptation is in large measure to be understood as the initial victory of God's King over the ancient foe, the devil. This is the opening salvo for the spread of the kingdom throughout the Gospels; by His obedience, Jesus is beginning to rein in the reign of the devil. The Gospels continue to trace this progressive advance of the kingdom in what follows.

The King Overcomes the Sins of the Past

By overcoming the devil, Jesus in His obedience reverses the course of the disobedience of Israel, Adam, and even David.

After the exodus, God's son was called out of Egypt, but in the wilderness, the Israelites groaned and complained. They did not prove to be the obedient sons they were called to be (Deut. 8:5–6). The people were idolatrous, so instead of enjoying the blessings of security and peace in the promised land, they faced opposition, division, and eventually exile. Jesus' obedience in the wilderness, where He, too, was tempted as the Son of God, is the obedience of the true Israel. By His obedience a greater, lasting peace in a greater, lasting promised land is secured—everlasting life.

Jesus' obedience also overcomes the sin of David. Like David when he was newly anointed king, Jesus was anointed and sent into the wilderness (see Mark 1:12). But Jesus is also unlike David because David's rule did not last forever. As great as David was, he was also a sinful man. David's sins are well known; in his lowest moment, he had one of his most capable and loyal men, Uriah the Hittite, murdered and took Uriah's wife as his own. This greatly displeased the Lord, and David repented. But David's kingdom never fully recovered, as he faced opposition from his son Absalom, who sought to usurp the throne. Matthew's genealogy, which focuses on David in a positive light (see Matt. 1:1, 17), also contains a subtle critique of David. Maybe you have noticed that four women are mentioned in Matthew's genealogy (Tamar, Rahab, Bathsheba, and Mary). This is true, but it is noteworthy that Matthew does not list Bathsheba's name. Instead, Matthew 1:6 states that "David was the father of Solomon by the wife of Uriah." In other words, David fathered Solomon by another man's wife. David's sin led to difficulty and instability in his kingdom; Jesus' obedience leads to the permanence of the eternal kingdom of God.

We can go even further. Jesus' obedience does not merely overcome Israel's and David's disobedience; the Gospels also present Jesus as the new Adam whose obedience secures the eternal life that Adam's disobedience forfeited. In the beginning Adam was offered eternal life in the context of God's covenant if he would obey perfectly from the heart. But if he failed this requirement, he would face death (see Gen. 2:17). We know the tragic outcome of Adam's fall, but Jesus comes as a new Adam who obeys where Adam disobeyed and by whose obedience we have eternal life by faith.

Mark's temptation account helps us see this Adamic dimension, for Mark writes that Jesus was with the wild animals (Mark 1:13).

The peaceful presence of Jesus with the wild animals assumes that His obedience is recovering the peace between people and animals that was true in Adam's day in the beginning but that was forfeited by Adam's sin. Adam was made in the image of God and was therefore a royal image bearer of God.[2] He was to reign over God's creation as a royal vicegerent, but Adam sinned and fell short of the glory of God (Rom. 3:23). Jesus' obedience as the second and last Adam—in the temptation and elsewhere—overcomes Adam's sin. Whereas one man's disobedience brought death, so one man's obedience brings life (5:18).

The temptation accounts of the Gospels show us the obedience of the King and set us up to find a clash of kingdoms elsewhere in them. Jesus' obedience is that of a public figure, the representative of His people. Whereas sin brings death, Jesus' obedience yields life.

The King's Message

Just after the significant encounter between Jesus and the devil, the Gospels speak of the coming of the kingdom of God. Jesus' ministry begins in this way: "Now after John was arrested, Jesus came into Galilee, proclaiming the gospel of God, and saying, 'The time is fulfilled, and the kingdom of God is at hand; repent and believe in the gospel'" (Mark 1:14–15). Notice twice in these verses that the word "gospel" is used, and these uses form a sort of bracket around the mention of the kingdom of God:

gospel of God → kingdom of God ← gospel

2 See also Patrick Schreiner, *The Kingdom of God and the Glory of the Cross*, Short Studies in Biblical Theology (Crossway, 2018), 30–33.

Mark is helping us see that the *gospel* is specifically the gospel *of the kingdom*. The term "kingdom" clarifies the nature of the gospel; they refer to the same reality.

Further support that the message of the gospel is the message of the kingdom comes from the Old Testament background for the term *gospel*. The phrase "the time is fulfilled" points to the time of the fulfillment of prophecy and God's plan of salvation. The great day of the Lord's redemption of His people was at hand, as it had been promised. John the Baptist was the voice crying in the wilderness, hailing the coming day of peace and forgiveness for God's suffering people (see Isa. 40:1–5). A new day of redemption was at hand, and this was good news for God's people.

In fact, the term *gospel* most likely finds its background in the prophet Isaiah. A few verses later in Isaiah 40, the good news is explained:

> Go on up to a high mountain,
>   O Zion, herald of good news;
> lift up your voice with strength,
>   O Jerusalem, herald of good news;
>   lift it up, fear not;
> say to the cities of Judah,
>   "Behold your God!"
> Behold, the Lord God comes with might,
>   and his arm rules for him;
> behold, his reward is with him,
>   and his recompense before him.
> He will tend his flock like a shepherd;
>   he will gather the lambs in his arms;

> he will carry them in his bosom,
> and gently lead those that are with young. (vv. 9–11)

The herald is to announce the good news, or gospel. This good news is focused on the Lord's mighty rescue of His people and His tender and protective shepherding of them. In Scripture, "shepherd" is often a royal image, for David was a shepherd, and the long-awaited King would shepherd God's people (see Ezek. 34:23; see also Matt. 9:36). The good news is that God's kingship will be manifest, and He will rule over His people and care for them.

Another mention of *gospel* in Isaiah comes in Isaiah 52:7:

> How beautiful upon the mountains
> are the feet of him who brings good news,
> who publishes peace, who brings good news of happiness,
> who publishes salvation,
> who says to Zion, "Your God reigns."

Again, the good news is of the kingship of God, whose power accomplishes salvation for His people. And this is good news not only for Israel but for all people (Isa. 60:6).

Isaiah 61:1–2 also speaks of the good news, and Jesus quotes this passage at the outset of His ministry in Luke 4:18–19:

> The Spirit of the Lord is upon me,
> because he has anointed me
> to proclaim good news to the poor.
> He has sent me to proclaim liberty to the captives
> and recovering of sight to the blind,

> to set at liberty those who are oppressed,
> to proclaim the year of the Lord's favor.

Jesus was anointed with the Holy Spirit for gospel preaching. The good news of Isaiah 61 relates to the final freedom for God's people who were in captivity. Using the Year of Jubilee as a background (Lev. 25), when all the debts of the people were forgiven, in Luke 4 Jesus speaks about final, full forgiveness of sins, echoing the way Isaiah 61 looked back to Leviticus 25. Here again, the "time is fulfilled," and God is intervening on behalf of His people. God's kingdom is coming (cf. Isa. 61:4).

Elsewhere Luke clearly relates the preaching of the good news to the message of the kingdom (Luke 4:43; 8:1; 16:16). One of the clearest texts relating the kingdom to the gospel is perhaps one of the most familiar passages from Luke: "And the angel said to them, 'Fear not, for behold, I bring you good news of great joy that will be for all the people. For unto you is born this day in the city of David a Savior, who is Christ the Lord'" (2:10–11). The good news that the angel brings to the shepherds outside Bethlehem is the birth of a King—Christ (the Messiah), the Son of David, who is born in the city of David. And as we saw in Matthew 1:21, this King will save His people from their sins. This is good news indeed. Peter makes a similar point in the book of Acts when he tells the Roman centurion Cornelius that Jesus preached good news of peace and that He is Lord of all (Acts 10:36). As scholars have often noted, calling Jesus "Lord of all" was a direct threat to Caesar, who would have been viewed incorrectly as "Lord of all."[3] The good news of peace comes

3 See C. Kavin Rowe, *World Upside Down: Reading Acts in the Graeco-Roman Age* (Oxford University Press, 2009), 112.

through the true King over all—Jesus Christ of Nazareth, the true Son of David.

I hope you're beginning to see the connection between the gospel and the kingdom. The gospel is about forgiveness of sins. The Gospels make this clear. For example, in Mark 1:14–15 the proper response to the gospel of the kingdom is to repent. In Isaiah 52:7, the good news is that "your God reigns," and this is described as a message of peace and salvation. Further, in Isaiah 40:9 the good news is closely related to the comfort for the people that their iniquity is pardoned in verses 1–2. The people's sins are not the last word, but the Lord would overcome the people's sin by delivering them from the consequences of their sins. It is important, therefore, to turn from sin and trust in God, who offers a way out. The coming of the kingdom of God means that the final King has come, and He is winning a victory that yields true, lasting forgiveness of sins.

In sum, the good news of the kingdom is both something Jesus tells us about and something that is focused on Jesus Himself. The gospel is both *about* Christ and *preached by* Christ. This "both-and" approach to the gospel is present in the first verse of Mark: "The beginning of the gospel of Jesus Christ, the Son of God." Scholars have often debated the question of what "*of* Jesus Christ" means. Does this refer to the gospel that is *about* Jesus Christ—that is, the gospel focused on Jesus Himself? Or does "of" refer to the gospel that is *preached by* Jesus Christ?

We have already seen examples of both: Jesus preaches the good news of the kingdom of God. So the gospel message must be something that is proclaimed verbally through the ministry of Christ. In fact, Jesus explicitly states that He has come to preach the gospel of the kingdom (Luke 4:43; see also Mark 1:38). Preaching was central to Jesus' ministry.

But Jesus is also the focus of the gospel message; the gospel is the good news about Jesus and what He does for us. This means the gospel is about the obedience of Christ—His miracles, His death, His resurrection, and all that He does in the Gospels. The kingdom is present where Jesus is present (Luke 17:20–21). The good news of the kingdom of God is good news about Jesus. Jesus' work on our behalf is good news, and by His work He brings the kingdom of God that we are called to be a part of.

Practical Takeaways

1. The message of the gospel must be related to the message of the kingdom. Jesus is the King of the kingdom whose work we benefit from by faith.
2. Jesus is not only our model for faithfulness in this world; He is also our representative and substitute. His obedience saves all those who look to Him in faith. His obedience includes not just His death on the cross (though it certainly includes that) but also His entire life of faithful obedience.
3. The gospel message must not be separated from Jesus. In our understanding of the gospel and our presentations of it, we must keep the focus on Christ. Jesus didn't just preach the gospel; the gospel itself is about Him.

5

The Timing of the Kingdom

I enjoy Christmas music and am happy to start listening to it as early as possible in the year (normally around October, but sometimes a bit sooner). I enjoy the rich theological hymns of Christmas. One of my other favorites is "Christmas Time Is Here" by the Vince Guaraldi Trio, made famous in *A Charlie Brown Christmas*. It's a song that I often associate with the Christmas season. Yet the season of "Christmas time" is over before you know it. When January rolls around, we look at Christmas in the rearview mirror. Christmas time is no longer here. We may be disappointed that we must wait another year for Christmas time to come again—and another year before listening to the great Christmas hymns!

The kingdom is not quite like that. It's not just something that came in the past that we look back and marvel at. Nor is the kingdom something that we can only look forward to in the future. Instead, the kingdom is a present reality; it is already here because Christ announced it during His earthly ministry, as we saw in the previous chapter.

In this chapter, I consider three aspects of the timing of the kingdom: its inauguration, its growth, and its future consummation. I will then relate this to how we are to pray in the Lord's Prayer, which is a prayer befitting the kingdom of God.

The Already–Not Yet Kingdom

I mentioned in chapter 1 that the past couple of hundred years have seen a fair amount of debate about the timing of the kingdom. Some have argued that the kingdom is something entirely in the past. Others have seen the kingdom as something entirely in the future. Both extremes can miss the importance of recognizing that the kingdom has already arrived during the ministry of Jesus.

It is now more commonly recognized that the kingdom of God is *already* here in an important sense. It is here because Christ inaugurated the kingdom during His earthly ministry. I mentioned this in the previous chapter, and I will have much more to say about this in future chapters. The kingdom comes because Christ has come. He has inaugurated the kingdom. It is also true that the kingdom is *not yet* here in all its fullness as it will be when Christ returns. There remains a future fulfillment for the kingdom, which I will discuss more fully in chapter 15. Christ will return in the future, and this will be the time of the kingdom's majestic consummation.

We presently find ourselves in the interim period between the first coming of Christ and His second coming. This interim period may seem unremarkable from an earthly perspective, but in reality, we are living in the time between the ages when the kingdom has *already* come in one sense but is *not yet* here fully. This is what is often called the already–not yet structure of New Testament theology. The great blessings of the kingdom anticipated by the prophets to come "in the latter days" have already begun to be realized because Christ has come and has ascended. Note, for example, how Peter explains that the blessings of "the latter days" (Acts 2:17) prophesied by Joel have become a reality on the day of Pentecost (vv. 17–21, citing Joel 2:28–32). The phrase "latter days" is a way the Old Testament prophets spoke about the coming age of blessing (e.g., Isa. 2:2; Dan. 2:28; Hos. 3:5; Mic. 4:1; see also Gen. 49:1; Deut. 4:30; Joel 2:28). Those days have truly arrived.

At the same time, not every blessing of the latter days is here in fullness. Even though the kingdom has *already* come, it is *not yet* here in all its fullness. For example, though Christ reigns over the kingdom, we still suffer, we still sin, and we still encounter many enemies of God and His people in the world. One day those will be overcome when Christ returns and consummates His kingdom. But that day still lies in the future.

We can set forth the timing of the kingdom's coming in the following way:

> *Inauguration*: Christ inaugurated the kingdom during His earthly ministry and especially by His death, resurrection, and ascension.
>
> *Growth*: We currently live in the in-between time of the growth of the kingdom. The kingdom will continue to grow until the consummation, but that growth may often seem hidden in the eyes of the world (see Matt. 13:24–30).
>
> *Consummation*: The future consummation of the kingdom will come when Christ returns.

This means that the kingdom is truly here, but there remains a future escalation of the kingdom. We live "in the meantime," which means that we live in the light of the kingdom that has come and continues to grow, but we look ahead by faith to the full, open reign of Christ that will come.

To understand the already–not yet character of the kingdom, we can compare it to World War II's D-Day.[1] D-Day was the decisive day when the Allied armed forces successfully entered Europe, ultimately ensuring the defeat of the Nazis. Once the Allies landed successfully, they brought more and more men and materiel ashore and gained the foothold they needed to win the European war. This did not, however, ensure an immediate end to the war. Battles still had to be fought and won. The war in Europe continued for close to a year, and many people tragically lost their lives. Even so, the invasion of D-Day was the decisive moment ensuring Allied victory.

In a similar way, when Christ came to earth to inaugurate the kingdom, it was like D-Day's ensuring the final victory. Christ's initial coming did not bring the final consummation of the kingdom, but in the present age His kingdom continues to advance and grow, and in the future Christ will return and bring a new day of peace.

The Prayer of the Kingdom

The prayer that Jesus taught His disciples to pray, which we commonly call the Lord's Prayer (Matt. 6:9–13; see also Luke 11:2–4),

1 See also Oscar Cullmann, *Christ and Time: The Primitive Christian Conception of Time and History*, trans. Floyd V. Filson, rev. ed. (Westminster, 1964), 83–87, 141–46.

is a kingdom prayer. It assumes the coming of the kingdom through Christ and shows us how we ought to pray now considering the kingdom realities in which we live. Jesus tells His disciples:

> "Pray then like this:
>
> "Our Father in heaven,
> hallowed be your name.
> Your kingdom come,
> your will be done,
>   on earth as it is in heaven.
> Give us this day our daily bread,
> and forgive us our debts,
>   as we also have forgiven our debtors.
> And lead us not into temptation,
>   but deliver us from evil." (Matt. 6:9–13)

When we pray "our Father," we are reminded that we can call God Father because of what Christ has done for us; through Christ we can call God Father (see Heidelberg Catechism 120). When we pray "our Father in heaven," we are reminded of the majesty and authority of God, the heavenly King who can give us what we need (see HC 121).

The first petition of the Lord's Prayer is "Hallowed be your name." This is a prayer for God to be glorified, which is also important in the context of the kingdom; the kingdom of God is ultimately about the glory of God. When we pray "Hallowed be your name," we are praying a kingdom prayer that God's name and glory would be exalted in the earth. In his classic book, Herman Ridderbos comments on this petition: "The coming of the kingdom is first of all the display of the divine glory."[2]

The second and third petitions of the Lord's Prayer are also related to the kingdom: "Your kingdom come, your will be done, on earth as it is in heaven." Richard Pratt has observed, "This prayer sums up the central message of the Bible in a few words."[3] This is a prayer that God's kingdom would come more and more fully and that God's will would be done on earth. In this case "will of God" means doing what God commands.[4] It is also a prayer that God's kingdom would be extended throughout the world. Heidelberg Catechism 123 captures the second petition memorably:

> "Your kingdom come" means: Rule us by your Word and Spirit in such a way that more and more we submit to you. Preserve and increase your church. Destroy the devil's work; destroy every force which revolts against you and every conspiracy against your holy Word. Do all this until your kingdom fully comes, when you will be all in all.[5]

Another helpful exposition of the second petition comes from Westminster Larger Catechism 191. Among other things, the Larger Catechism says that in this petition "we pray that the kingdom of sin

---

2 Ridderbos, *Coming of the Kingdom*, 20–21; see also Vos, *Teaching of Jesus*, 11, 20–21, 49, 51.

3 Pratt, *Designed for Dignity*, 3–4.

4 Kevin DeYoung, *The Lord's Prayer: Learning from Jesus on What, Why, and How to Pray* (Crossway, 2022), 46–47.

5 Translation from Chad Van Dixhoorn, ed., *Creeds, Confessions, and Catechisms: A Reader's Edition* (Crossway, 2022).

and Satan may be destroyed, the gospel propagated throughout the world . . . : that Christ would rule in our hearts here." This is also a prayer that the church would be strengthened in this age. Praying for God's kingdom to come is to pray for God's will to be done on earth in the present age as we look ahead to the second coming of Christ.

We are also to pray, "Lead us not into temptation." It is especially important to understand the timing of the kingdom's coming to understand this petition. Put simply, this is a prayer that we be spared the wiles and traps of the devil that would lead us into sin even now. This is a practical prayer for daily living.

In contemporary scholarship, however, it has become common to view this prayer as a very specific prayer about being spared from the great *trial* or *tribulation* (the Greek term *peirasmos* can mean either of these, as well as the more familiar *temptation*) at the end of time.[6] Despite the popularity of this view, this narrower reading of being delivered from the final eschatological trial misses the present reality of kingdom conflict around us every day and that the kingdom does not come all at once.[7] We need to be spared the snares of the devil, for right now he roams around like a roaring lion (1 Peter 5:8). This is not just a prayer for the future; it is a prayer for faithful kingdom living each day.

The interim between the first and second comings of Christ is a time when the devil's kingdom is defeated in principle, but the devil is still active. We live in a time of continuing spiritual danger. As we

---

6 E.g., Ernst Lohmeyer, *"Our Father": An Introduction to the Lord's Prayer*, trans. John Bowden (Harper & Row, 1965), 195, 203–6; and Raymond E. Brown, "The Pater Noster as an Eschatological Prayer," *Theological Studies* 22 (1961): 205.

7 See Vos, *Teaching of Jesus*, 36; see also Ridderbos, *Coming of the Kingdom*, 107–8.

will see further in chapter 7, we live in a time of conflict between kingdoms. We therefore need to be protected in this age of kingdom growth that we may come safely into the consummated kingdom in the future. We therefore must pray that we are not led into temptation but are delivered from evil and from the evil one himself.

The text of the Lord's Prayer in Matthew does not include the traditional ending that is part of the liturgical use of the Lord's Prayer: "For Thine is the kingdom, and the power, and the glory forever. Amen." This portion of the prayer is not found in the best manuscripts but most likely comes from the end of David's prayer in 1 Chronicles 29:11. It therefore is most certainly a biblical prayer, and it is appropriate to pray in conjunction with the Lord's Prayer. Jesus is the greater David who brings a greater kingdom. If David could pray that the kingdom belongs to the Lord forever, surely it is appropriate for us to pray this, since Christ has brought the long-awaited kingdom promised in Scripture.

Practical Takeaways

1. We can be thankful that Christ has brought the kingdom and it will be consummated in the future. We presently live in the in-between time of difficulty and struggle, yet we should be encouraged that this is also the time of the growth of the kingdom. We must continue to move forward by faith, considering the kingdom's certain future success.
2. Prayer is crucial in this time of growth. As we pray for God's kingdom to come, we should pray that our own lives will increasingly conform to God's revealed will. One of the glories of the kingdom is the way that redeemed sinners turn from sin and live in ways that reflect God's character.
3. Let us, by God's grace, seek to magnify His glory in our lives, and let us pray to this end. Seeking God's glory in all that we do is consistent with the goal of the kingdom.

6

The Signs of the Kingdom

We live in a world with many divisions—political affiliations, regional and national loyalties, sports teams, favorite product brands. We approach things in terms of division even in school; math, history, science, literature, and social studies are all considered different topics with different teachers. Colleges have separate departments for these disciplines, and even within the same discipline there are diverging specializations and areas of interest.

But we must not lose the biblical perspective that life is integrated. We too quickly divide what should be kept together. The entire world is God's world, and Jesus is a holistic Savior. God created the world good, and this includes the physical aspects of creation and our physical bodies. But the great tragedy of sin that came with Adam has led to negative consequences throughout God's good creation. Sin affects not just our souls but the physical world, including our physical bodies. It is not good for the physical world to be marred in imperfection. We need sin in all its consequences to be overcome.

In this chapter, we will look at Jesus' miracles and how they are kingdom works that overcome the effects of sin holistically. In the beginning, God created the world good, without sin. He was the great King over the world, and Adam was the royal image bearer designed to spread God's glory. Adam's failure affected all his posterity and the entire world. Adam's sin broke fellowship with God, introduced death into the world, and led to the cursing of the physical world as well.

As our Savior, Jesus comes to restore and advance God's kingdom in ways that overcome all the effects of the fall into sin—physical as well as spiritual. Miracles are not simply impressive works that show the power of Jesus; they are also ways that the kingdom of God advances. They manifest the restoration of creation and move the world toward new creation.

Miracles as Kingdom Works

Unity of Word and Deed

There are so many specific miracles that Jesus accomplishes in the Gospels that it can sometimes be easy to miss the big picture. It is fine to read each miracle story on its own, but we must not miss the overarching purpose of Jesus' miracles more holistically. To understand miracles well, we need to integrate them into the flow of the narratives of the Gospels.

One of the important principles of Jesus' ministry is the unity of word ministry and deed ministry. Jesus does not *either* preach the gospel *or* perform miracles; He does both. Jesus does not meet *either* the spiritual needs of people *or* their physical needs; He meets both.

This holistic emphasis is seen in Jesus' healing a paralytic in Mark 2:1–12. In this account, a man who was unable to walk was carried to Jesus by four men. When they were unable to get access to Jesus because of the large crowd, they went to the roof of the house, removed a portion of it, and let the man down on a mat. Jesus' initial statement to the man may not be what we expect: "Son, your sins are forgiven" (v. 5). We are probably right to conclude that the paralytic was coming to Jesus to be healed. But the man's persistence also revealed true faith in Jesus, which was able to make the man entirely whole.

In this case, Jesus first tells the man that his sins are forgiven. Then, to demonstrate His authority to forgive sins (which only God can do), Jesus healed the man so that he was able to get up and walk. Jesus made the man both physically and spiritually whole. This holistic healing is probably the same unified healing that the Apostle James has in view when he writes that the Lord can heal those who pray as well as forgive their sins (James 5:13–16). This reflects the unity of physical and spiritual healing in the ministry of Jesus.

One of the debated issues about the kingdom of God and its application today is what the balance should be between word ministry and deed ministry. Here we can make two opposing errors. On the one hand, we could so emphasize the spiritual message of the gospel that we lose sight of the holistic message of the kingdom for those in need. Another error is to emphasize meeting the physical needs of people so much that we neglect the message of the kingdom.

We should learn from Jesus, in whose ministry word and deed coexisted harmoniously. Jesus healed people both spiritually and physically. And in at least one context we can see how Jesus ensured that the message of the kingdom was not obscured by a multitude of miraculous works (Mark 1:37–39).[1] Jesus is a holistic Savior, and the kingdom message is of the good news that sin in all its consequences is being overcome through Christ.

Miracles and the Spread of the Kingdom

Jesus' miracles are therefore also ways that the kingdom of God spreads; where the consequences of sin are overcome in the physical realm, there the kingdom of God advances against sin and its effects. The miracles of the kingdom bring restoration that reflects the original creation. In the beginning, Adam and Eve had perfect, harmonious dominion over the natural realm, and there were no thorns and thistles with which to contend. The miracles of the kingdom overcome sin and provide glimpses of untainted creation. But more than that, the miracles propel us toward a glorious new creation. Miracles restore life and mark the kingdom of God, which is characterized by abundant life.

One of the ways that we can see that the kingdom of God is a kingdom of fullness of life is to look at the Gospel of John. Matthew, Mark, and Luke share many of the same stories about Jesus, but John includes several different stories and slightly different emphases from the other three Gospels. That is not to say that John contradicts the others. Instead, John often brings out in a distinctive way the implications of what is taught in the other Gospels. "Kingdom" is one of the concepts for which John provides a slightly different angle.

In Matthew, Mark, and Luke, Jesus often speaks about the kingdom, but only rarely in John does Jesus mention the kingdom. Instead, John provides something like a commentary on the meaning

1 See Ridderbos, *Coming of the Kingdom*, 115–21.

of the kingdom by emphasizing life in Christ. For example, Jesus says in John, "I came that they may have life and have it abundantly" (10:10). And in the famous John 3:16, which comes in one of only two contexts in John where the kingdom is mentioned explicitly (see 3:5), Jesus says that all who believe in the only begotten Son of God have eternal life.

Life in Christ comes where the kingdom is spread, and that life is the richness of eternal life that we experience even now. Where Jesus does miraculous works, He spreads the kingdom and restores life to a world in need. We can even say that miracles reflect the fullness of life that constitutes the kingdom of God.

Some examples illustrate this close relationship of the kingdom to life. The paralytic's restoration to physical health recalls the original creation design for people to stand and walk on two legs. The restoration of sight to those who were blind restores the original design for our eyes to see the beauty of God's world. Often Jesus' miracles reverse the course of death: cleansing from a serious skin disorder (often translated as "leprosy"), which was like living with a constant reminder of death on the skin; healing the woman with a bleeding disorder; and raising people from the dead. Death is an intrusion into God's good creation. Jesus' various ways of overcoming death reverse the atrophic slide toward it and offer a recalibration and restoration toward life. Miracles are ways that the kingdom of life advances in a world of sin.

Miracles as Signs of the Kingdom

In addition to marking the spread of the kingdom, miracles illustrate the character of the kingdom. They show us the full-orbed life of the kingdom of God. In this sense, miracles can be understood as signs of the kingdom. They demonstrate what the kingdom is like. Here again, the Gospel of John adds clarity to the miracles in all four Gospels. In John, miracles are explicitly called "signs," indicating their role in showing us the nature of Jesus and His kingdom. Scholars debate the number and nature of signs in John, but the best view is that the signs are all miraculous in John, and there are seven signs, indicating completeness in Christ. John includes fewer miracles (or "signs") than the other Gospels, but he seems to select and arrange his narrative around the most impressive and strategic signs for his purposes.[2] These seven signs are structured so that they lead us to understand the importance of the death and resurrection of Christ.

One of the clearest examples in this regard is the raising of Lazarus in John 11. Raising Lazarus is not simply a miracle that demonstrates the love of Christ for Lazarus and his family. Nor is the raising of Lazarus simply a way for Jesus to show people His power. The miracle does both of these things: It really meets the needs of hurting people, and it really does show us the power of Jesus. But there is another angle here as well: The raising of Lazarus foreshadows Jesus' resurrection from the dead later in the Gospel of John. Jesus has already said that He has the power to lay down His life and the power to take it up again (John 10:17–18), and in the raising of Lazarus in John 11, Jesus shows us that He does indeed have the power to raise the dead. To understand rightly the raising of Lazarus is to understand it in relation to Christ's death and resurrection and to the everlasting kingdom that He brings.

---

2 In my view, the seven signs are (1) turning water into wine, (2) healing a nobleman's son, (3) healing a lame man in Jerusalem, (4) feeding the five thousand, (5) healing a blind man in Jerusalem, (6) raising Lazarus, and (7) Jesus' own glorification (i.e., death and resurrection).

In sum, to understand the signs in John, we must understand how they reveal Christ. In fact, the purpose statement of the Gospel of John focuses on the importance of the signs for understanding Christ:

> Now Jesus did many other signs in the presence of the disciples, which are not written in this book; but these [signs] are written so that you may believe that Jesus is the Christ, the Son of God, and that by believing you may have life in his name. (20:30–31)

This means that to understand the miracles in John—and, indeed, the miracles in all four Gospels—we need to read them in context. The miracles are not deeds disconnected from the overall kingdom message of Jesus. Instead, they enact and illustrate that kingdom message in singularly impressive ways. The miracles show us what the fullness of life looks like in the kingdom.

Jesus' miracles also attest that the kingdom has arrived. While the kingdom may be largely invisible to us, that does not mean that it is not here (as we will see later in a chapter on Jesus' parables). The power of miracles reflects the powerful entrance of God's kingdom into our world.

The role of miracles as signs is closely related to the role of miracles as anticipations of the fuller coming of the kingdom in the future. Though Jesus healed many who were sick and in need of help, He did not heal everyone. Though He healed a leper, others were not healed. Though He healed some who were blind, others were not healed. Not everyone experienced then (or experiences now) a miracle in this age, even though the kingdom has truly come. But miracles demonstrate to us the future reality of what the kingdom will look like when it comes in all its fullness and when sin and its destructive effects will finally be overcome. We can therefore be encouraged today by the miracles that occurred back then.

In the future, when Christ returns, there will be no more imperfections in our bodies, no more terror of the sea, no more uncleanliness. All will be whole. The miracles that Jesus accomplished in this age point us forward to the coming age of resurrection glory.

The Bread of Life

To pursue this line of thinking further, I will consider Jesus' feeding of the five thousand in the wilderness—a miracle recorded in all four Gospels. This is an extremely significant event in the Gospels, and it is dripping with kingdom implications. The context is important:

> And Jesus went throughout all the cities and villages, teaching in their synagogues and proclaiming the gospel of the kingdom and healing every disease and every affliction. When he saw the crowds, he had compassion for them, because they were harassed and helpless, like sheep without a shepherd. (Matt. 9:35–36)

Jesus has been preaching and enacting the kingdom through miraculous works (see also Luke 9:11). Further, Jesus notices that the people are like sheep without a shepherd, which alludes to the Old Testament language of "shepherd" for kingship (1 Kings 22:17; Ezek. 34:5). Jesus will prove to be the royal messianic Shepherd to instruct and provide for the people.

Mark and John also relate Jesus' feeding of the five thousand to His kingship. In Mark, this account of the feeding comes just after the feast of King Herod Antipas, where Herod's ungodly kingship and ungodly feasting led to the death of John the Baptist (Mark 6:14–29).[3] Jesus' kingship and provision are therefore contrasted with that of King Herod. Similarly, in John 6, after Jesus feeds the five thousand, the people want to make Jesus king by force (v. 15). While Jesus is indeed the true messianic King, His kingship looks different from many popular expectations in His day. Further, just as Ezekiel 34:11–16 anticipates the coming day when the Lord would be the people's Shepherd, so Nehemiah's prayer thanks the Lord for His provision of bread in the wilderness (Neh. 9:15). Jesus does the works of God. Jesus is the divine messianic King; He is not only David's Son, but also David's Lord.

Jesus therefore does not just speak of the provision of earthly bread, but uses this earthly bread as a sign to point to His role as the Bread of Life. This is clearest in John, where Jesus explains the meaning of the multiplication of bread in the wilderness: Jesus is the true Bread come down from heaven who gives life to the world (John 6:33–40). The main point to understand from the wilderness feeding is not simply that Christ can provide bread but that He is the ultimate provision for us. We should see His mighty works and put our trust in the One who sustains us more than perishable bread ever could. We should be united to Christ by faith and remain in Him. The provision of bread helps us understand what it means to abide in Christ (see John 6:56).

Similarly, in Mark Jesus draws His disciples' attention to the number of baskets of leftovers after He fed five thousand (twelve) and then again after He fed four thousand (seven). He wants them

3 Helen K. Bond, *The First Biography of Jesus: Genre and Meaning in Mark's Gospel* (Eerdmans, 2020), 185–86.

to understand about the bread and rebukes them for not understanding (Mark 6:52; 8:14–21).[4] What was it about the bread that He wanted them to understand? Presumably that the bread was about more than just bread; it was about the power and presence of Christ with His disciples. Jesus will later build on this imagery in the Last Supper, where the bread represents His body. The meaning of the bread in this context builds on the presence of bread earlier in the gospel, including the miraculous role of bread in the feeding of the five thousand.

One further use of bread is illuminating. In the Lord's Prayer, we ask our Father to give us our daily bread (Matt. 6:11). This petition is certainly a request for our physical needs to be met. But it is revealing that in the history of interpretation, this prayer has sometimes been understood as a prayer to be filled with Christ Himself—the true Bread of heaven. Again, it is helpful to remember that in God's world the spiritual and the physical should not be dichotomized. Yes, we need to pray for our daily sustenance. But ultimately that daily sustenance should remind us that our greatest need is to be filled with Christ Himself. He is the Bread of Life.

4 See also William L. Lane, *The Gospel According to Mark*, New International Commentary on the New Testament (Eerdmans, 1974), 238.

Practical Takeaways

1. God's creation is good, but it has been marred by sin. The miracles of Jesus in the Gospels remind us of this goodness of creation and point us ahead to the day when sin and its effects will be overcome. To this end, we should also have a holistic outlook on life and ministry that does not sharply dichotomize between the spiritual and the physical.
2. John's gospel helps us understand that the kingdom is about life—fullness of life. One of the best commentaries on the kingdom is to understand it as the realm of full life in Christ.
3. Jesus is the Bread of Life, and our life is found in Him. Let us always remember that the kingdom message should point us to Christ, who is our Redeemer. We live by faith in Him in this kingdom.

7

The Clash of Kingdoms

As I mentioned in chapter 2, much of the Old Testament is about the ups and downs of God's kingdom. These ups and downs are because of the people's sins and the opposition of other kingdoms against God's kingdom: the Moabites, Egyptians, Amalekites, Midianites, Philistines, Assyrians, Babylonians, Medo-Persians, and Greeks. These are some of the kingdoms arrayed against God's people in the Old Testament. These were real threats, and deliverance from these enemies was true deliverance for God's people.

But deliverance from these kingdoms was not final deliverance. The people still sinned, and their sins still led to consequences—most dramatically in the exile. For final deliverance to come and God's kingdom to be established fully and finally, the ultimate enemy must be defeated. This enemy is bigger than any earthly kingdom; this is the enemy who lies behind all of God's enemies. Jesus had to defeat the devil (1 John 3:8). For lasting deliverance to come and for God's kingdom to be firmly established, Jesus must overcome the kingdom of darkness that has taken root in our world. The Seed of the woman had to come and defeat the serpent.

The Gospels narrate this cosmic battle. We have seen it already in the temptation account where Jesus, as the representative for God's people, overcomes the devil through His true obedience. From this point in the Gospels, the kingdom progressively spreads further and further through the obedience and powerful work of Christ. This will lead us in due course to a discussion of the death and resurrection of Jesus (see especially chapters 14–15), but even before these climactic events, Jesus overcomes the kingdom of the devil throughout His ministry.

In this chapter, we will look at two major issues. First, we will look at the explanation Jesus gives about His victory over the devil and how this is related to the forgiveness of sins, particularly in Mark 3:22–30. Second, we will consider some other ways that the kingdom advances in the Gospels, specifically in Matthew 10–11.

The Stronger Man's Kingdom

Jesus' Authority over the Demonic Realm

Among the miraculous works of Jesus in the Gospels are the exorcisms of demons. These accounts mark the conflict between the kingdom of God and the kingdom of the devil. The conflicts start early in His ministry. In the Gospel of Mark, in the first record of His teaching in the synagogue at Capernaum, Jesus cast out a demonic spirit from a possessed man (Mark 1:21–28).[1] Yet this demon was no match for Jesus, who silenced the demon and commanded it to come out of the man.

1 Mark calls it an unclean spirit, which is a demonic spirit.

Later, Jesus healed a man who was possessed by many demons. When asked his name, the man replied, "Legion, for we are many" (Mark 5:9). Though no one could tame this man who lived among the tombs, not even with chains and shackles, at the word of Jesus the demons left him. They continued their deadly ways by destroying a herd of pigs.

Such exorcisms are not isolated episodes disconnected from the larger, unified work of Christ in the Gospels. Instead, these should be understood as ways that the kingdom of God advances against the kingdom of the devil. The demons are agents of the devil's kingdom, and they had found a realm and an authority on earth—often even in the promised land! But Jesus came with a new authority, and where He commanded, the demons fled and the kingdom of God advanced.

It is also clear that this clash of kingdoms between Jesus and the demonic realm is not a case of two equal (but opposing) powers. By no means! The demons know that they are at the mercy of Jesus, and He vastly overpowers them. He has the authority to destroy them—even thousands of them; they are subject to His command, for He is the holy Son of God Most High (Mark 1:24; 3:11; 5:7). Where the demons reign, life is culled and death advances. This can be seen in the demon-possessed man who lived among the tombs and cut himself with rocks (5:3–5). But where the kingdom of God advances through the work of Christ, life ensues. The man who had a legion of demons was restored and no longer lived among the tombs. In turn, the demons possessed and overpowered a herd of pigs that drowned in the sea. While the economic loss of a herd of pigs would have been great, it was not as great as the loss of human life and dignity. Sin brings death and destruction; the kingdom of God brings life and wholeness.

The encounter with the man with a legion of demons also shows us that Jesus is the Stronger One predicted by John the Baptist (Mark 1:7). No one had been able to control this man. Yet Jesus proved stronger than the man who had overpowered everyone, whose strength had come from dark, supernatural forces. Jesus is the Stronger One who is more powerful than the kingdom of darkness. He sets this man free.

The Stronger Man Binds the Strong Man

We know that the demons represent the devil's kingdom because of the explanation that Jesus gives in Mark 3:22–30, which follows. This cryptic, parabolic passage is important in the Gospel of Mark, for it explains the theological significance of much of what has been happening in the narrative to this point.[2]

> And the scribes who came down from Jerusalem were saying, "He is possessed by Beelzebul," and "by the prince of demons he casts out the demons." And he called them to him and said to them in parables, "How can Satan cast out Satan? If a kingdom is divided against itself, that kingdom cannot stand. And if a house is divided against itself, that house will not be able to stand. And if Satan has risen up against himself and is divided, he cannot stand, but is coming to an end. But no one can enter a strong man's house and plunder his goods, unless he first binds the strong man. Then indeed he may plunder his house.

2 On this, see Elizabeth E. Shively, *Apocalyptic Imagination in the Gospel of Mark: The Narrative and Theological Role of Mark 3.22–30*, Beihefte zur Zeitschrift für die neutestamentliche Wissenschaft 189 (Walter de Gruyter, 2012), 1–2.

> "Truly, I say to you, all sins will be forgiven the children of man, and whatever blasphemies they utter, but whoever blasphemes against the Holy Spirit never has forgiveness, but is guilty of an eternal sin"—for they were saying, "He has an unclean spirit."

The context for this passage is set in Mark 3:22: The scribes from Jerusalem did not believe Jesus' message but ludicrously suggested that He was possessed by Beelzebul. This name may not be meaningful to us today, but in the first century this was a way to refer to the devil. These religious leaders were not denying the reality of Jesus' exorcisms; they were denying the source of His spiritual power. They were attributing His power over the demonic realm to the power of Satan. This was blasphemy!

Jesus responds to this accusation by contrasting His kingdom with the kingdom of the devil. Students of modern history may be familiar with the American president Abraham Lincoln's warning that a house divided against itself cannot stand. He was speaking about the inability of the United States to remain divided on the issue of slavery. But these words come from Jesus, and He uses them to refer to His attack on Satan's kingdom.

In verse 24, Jesus makes the point that a kingdom divided against itself cannot stand. Satan does not cast out Satan, for if he did, then his kingdom would implode and there would be no need for Jesus to oppose his kingdom. Jesus explains that, rather, His exorcisms are attacks on the kingdom of Satan. A house divided against itself would be a *kingdom* divided against itself. Jesus' exorcisms demonstrate that He is reigning in the kingdom of the devil, and He is not in league with the devil. It makes no sense for Jesus to be in partnership with

Satan, because Jesus' exorcisms are ways that the kingdom of the devil is being defeated.

Jesus then expands on His analogy. In verse 27, He compares the devil to a strong man who holds people in captivity. The only way that this strong man can be defeated is if a stronger man arrives who can overpower the strong man. In this analogy, Jesus is the stronger man, for this is exactly what John the Baptist prophesied of the coming Messiah. The Stronger One is Jesus (Mark 1:7), who overcomes the devil already in the temptation account (vv. 12–13) and continues to overcome the devil in His powerful ministry. The relationship of Jesus' kingdom authority in Mark 3:22–30 to His obedience in Mark 1:12–13 highlights that the kingdom of God comes through the work of the perfectly obedient Son of God.

This is good news, because the Stronger One plunders the strong man's house (Mark 3:27). To plunder the strong man's house means liberating those who are in bondage to the devil. To plunder the devil's kingdom means setting people free (see John 8:34–36).

This is also good news because the kingdom authority of Jesus leads to forgiveness of sins—to free people from the shackles of the strong man entails the forgiveness of sins. Here we need to pay careful attention to the relationship between Mark 3:27 and 28. In verse 27, Jesus says that the strong man's house is plundered when the strong man is bound. By restraining the demonic world and proving fully obedient, Jesus was binding the strong man. Notice in verse 28 Jesus says that all sins and blasphemies will be forgiven. Mark does not spell out the logical relationship between these two verses, but verse 28 seems to be the "therefore" building on verse 27. To paraphrase: *Because* Jesus binds the devil, *therefore* all sins and blasphemies will be forgiven. The parallel text in Matthew 12:31

makes this logic explicit: "Therefore I tell you, every sin and blasphemy will be forgiven." Jesus' kingdom authority also means that He has the authority to forgive our sins and bring us into His kingdom. Jesus has bound the strong man and has authority to forgive all sins and blasphemies. The Apostle Paul speaks of this in similar language, telling us what God has done for us: "He has delivered us from the domain of darkness and transferred us to the kingdom of his beloved Son, in whom we have redemption, the forgiveness of sins" (Col. 1:13–14).

In Luke's account of this same episode, Jesus states, "But if it is by the finger of God that I cast out demons, then the kingdom of God has come upon you" (Luke 11:20; see also Matt. 12:28). This coming of the kingdom was already being realized during the ministry of Jesus. This is probably what Jesus has in view in Luke 10:18–19 when He says that He saw Satan fall like lightning. This seems to refer to a new development in the advance of the kingdom of God, as the ministry of the disciples, including their authority over demonic spirits granted by Christ (see Luke 10:17), advanced against the kingdom of the devil. The authority of the disciples over the power of the enemy (v. 19) shows that the kingdom of God overcomes the kingdom of the devil. Jesus' casting out demons indicates that the long-awaited age of blessing has come; this is the age of the kingdom that correlates to Jesus' casting out demons as the Stronger One (see Matt. 12:28).

Though Mark 3 promises forgiveness of sins for all sins and blasphemies, it does leave one exception. There is no forgiveness for blasphemy against the Holy Spirit (v. 29). This is a sobering text that we must read in context. We may wonder, Have I committed this unpardonable sin? How can I know?

Thankfully, the text of Mark helps us understand what this sin is. It is stated twice in verses 22 and 30. In both these verses, which bookend the entire episode, to blaspheme against the Holy Spirit is to call Jesus' authority evil. It is, in sum, to reject Christ. It is to say that Jesus' power comes from the devil. This is not a description of those who seek to honor Christ and love Him but who do so imperfectly. This is a passage about deliberate rejection of Christ.

The good news in this text should not be missed: Because of Jesus' spiritual authority over the kingdom of the devil, all sins and blasphemies will be forgiven those who come to Him in faith.

The Kingdom of God Advances

A New Development

In one sense, God has always been the great King over the world and His people. In Psalm 145:10–13, David praises God for His glorious kingdom:

> All your works shall give thanks to you, O Lord,
> and all your saints shall bless you!
> They shall speak of the glory of your kingdom
> and tell of your power,
> to make known to the children of man your mighty deeds,
> and the glorious splendor of your kingdom.
> Your kingdom is an everlasting kingdom,
> and your dominion endures throughout all generations.

Yet there is also a manifestly new sense to the kingdom in the Gospels. Something is happening through Jesus that had not happened before. Despite opposition to God's kingdom, the kingdom is present and advancing in a new way through the ministry of Jesus.

The Kingdom and Our Highest Loyalty

As we have already seen, when the kingdom comes, a conflict of kingdoms follows. Jesus warns His disciples about this in Matthew 10. Jesus sends His disciples out on a kingdom mission as sheep amid wolves (vv. 5–16). They are to continue the kingdom work of Jesus by doing the works that He has done: healing the sick, raising the dead, and cleansing lepers (vv. 7–8). Despite this spread of the kingdom, they should not expect peace but conflict. Jesus' message is one that divides the closest of earthly relationships (vv. 17–22; cf. Mic. 7:5–7).

When the kingdom comes, it precipitates conflict. Those opposed to the kingdom try to stop it, and opposition could come from anywhere. Jesus' warnings do not undermine the continuing importance of physical family relationships. Later in Matthew, He will make it clear that the fifth commandment ("Honor your father and your mother") remains in effect even for those who have aged parents (15:1–9). But Jesus is warning that the kingdom may precipitate a division even within a person's family—something that would have been even more striking for those who (rightly) viewed familial relationships as crucially important. But the kingdom of God requires a higher loyalty, one that reckons with the significance of Jesus.

Our view of the kingdom will mirror our view of Jesus: Is He indeed the promised Messiah? Did He truly bring the long-awaited kingdom of God? So important is this question that Jesus clarifies that His true family is ultimately defined not by physical family ties but by obedience to the will of God. The account we considered in Mark 3:22–30, where Jesus explains His authority over the kingdom of the devil, is framed at the beginning and the end with a discussion of His family. In Mark 3:21, Jesus' family thought that He was out of His mind, and in verses 31–35 Jesus clarifies who His true family is—those who do the will of God (v. 35). Devotion to Jesus and His kingdom must take priority over all else—even when it is difficult.

The Kingdom Advances Through Christ

One of the most revealing passages about the advance of the kingdom during Jesus' ministry comes in Matthew 11:2–19. In this context, John the Baptist is languishing in prison for his opposition to King Herod's immorality, and he sends messengers to Jesus to ask if He is the promised Messiah (v. 3). Since one of the blessings of the messianic age is freedom for the captives (see Luke 4:18), John's messengers may have wondered whether Jesus was going to get John out of prison.

In response, Jesus tells John's messengers about the kingdom works that were taking place through His ministry: The blind see, the lame walk, lepers are cleansed, the deaf hear, and the dead are raised (Matt. 11:5). Jesus is indeed the promised Messiah, as these good works attest (cf. Isa. 35:5–7). In addition to the list of miracles, Jesus ends His summary of good works by observing that "the poor have good news preached to them" (Matt. 11:5).

This good news is the gospel, and that it is preached to the poor recalls the outset of Jesus' ministry, where Jesus related His gospel preaching to the poor to the release of captives (Luke 4:18). Though John was in prison, Jesus was indeed preaching the gospel of the kingdom, including ultimate release for the captives, as Isaiah 61 envisioned. But this ultimate release did not mean John would get out of prison in that age, for the conflict continued then and continues still today.

This leads Jesus to a discussion of the role of John the Baptist in salvation history and the ongoing conflict between the kingdom of God and opposition to the kingdom in this age:

> "Truly I say to you, there has not arisen anyone born of women greater than John the Baptist; but the least in the kingdom of heaven is greater than he. From the days of John the Baptist until now the kingdom of heaven forcefully advances, and violent people plunder it." (Matt. 11:11–12, author's translation)

Two features of this text are relevant for the present topic. First, in verse 11 Jesus states that there is no one greater than John among anyone born before John. This is a stunning statement. Enoch, Abraham, Sarah, Isaac, Rebekah, Jacob, Rachel, Joseph, Moses, Aaron, Deborah, Ruth, David, Solomon, Elijah, Esther—none of these is greater than John; he outshines them all. To what should we attribute John's incomparable greatness?

The answer must lie in John's position in redemptive history: John's greatness is seen in his relationship to the coming of the kingdom of God. Only John had the privilege of directly preparing the way for the coming of the long-promised Messiah—the Son of God Himself. John's greatness is seen in His proximity to Christ. Put simply, John's greatness is because of Christ's greatness. John's ministry leans forward from the old era and touches the new era of the final kingdom of God.

Second, notice that Jesus talks about the nature of conflict in this text. I have provided my own translation for these two verses because of the trickiness of translating verse 12 and the importance of that translation for how we understand the advance of the kingdom in this passage. The key question is whether the kingdom of heaven "forcefully advances," as I have translated it, or whether the kingdom of heaven "has suffered violence," as the ESV and many other fine translations render it. Either option is possible.

This is a difficult translational choice because "forcefully advances" and "has suffered violence" are the same word and form in Greek. One must choose from the context which translation is more fitting, and in this case both options work. It therefore takes a deeper dive into the context to choose between the two options.

In favor of "has suffered violence" is that Jesus speaks about violent people who try to stop the kingdom, and John is in prison for his kingdom commitment. With this view, the verb "has suffered violence" is understood more negatively, as is the reference to violent people: It is the violent people who attack the kingdom, and therefore it suffers violence.

Even so, I believe that the translation "forcefully advances" better fits the context of Matthew 11 (and the parallel passage in Luke 16:16). Jesus is speaking about how the kingdom of God is advancing through His ministry despite opposition. The text, therefore, presents a contrast between the advance of the kingdom and the violent people who try to plunder it.

Matthew 11:12 speaks of the advance of the kingdom of God through the ministry of Christ. Further supporting this is the likely Old Testament background from Micah 2:13:

He who opens the breach goes up before them;
they break through and pass the gate,
going out by it.
Their king passes on before them,
the LORD at their head.[3]

This passage in Micah looks forward to the time when the Davidic King, representing the Lord, would break through against His enemies.

That final King is Christ, through whom the kingdom advances despite opposition. In this age, the opposition to the kingdom will continue, but in the end, the kingdom of God will outlast all opposition.

Practical Takeaways

1. Evil is real. The world can be a scary place. But Jesus is more powerful than any evil force or being. We can't defeat the devil; Jesus does that. We are called to take refuge in Christ. By union with Christ through faith, we should put on the full armor of God, submitting ourselves to God and resisting the devil by faith.
2. Jesus is the One who can free us from the bondage of the devil. The devil keeps people in captivity, but Jesus

3 See R. Stephen Notley, "The Kingdom of Heaven Forcefully Advances," in *The Interpretation of Scripture in Early Judaism and Christianity: Studies in Language and Tradition*, ed. Craig A. Evans, Journal for the Study of the Pseudepigrapha Supplement Series 33 / Studies in Scripture in Early Judaism and Christianity 7 (Sheffield Academic, 2000), 305–6; and John Calvin, *Commentaries on the Twelve Minor Prophets*, trans. John Owen (Baker, 2003), 3:211.

binds the devil and frees those who are in captivity. Jesus has the authority to forgive all sins and blasphemies for those who come to Him. We've all done and said things that we wish we could take back. We can't change the past, but Jesus can forgive what is past for those who turn to Him and participate in His kingdom.

3. Jesus faced violent opposition in His day, and we can expect that the kingdom will continue to face opposition in this age. Sometimes it may even seem as if the kingdom has stalled or failed. But the kingdom will continue to progress until Jesus returns. In the end, the kingdom that may seem small and insignificant in the eyes of the world will turn out to be the most powerful, lasting kingdom that the world has ever seen.

8

The Parables of the Kingdom

Good teachers know how to communicate complex truths in a simple way. Anyone can make a complex subject sound complex; it takes a good teacher to make the complex simple. You may have noticed this in sermons; illustrations often bring a point to life and more easily impress the meaning of a text in our memory.

No one has ever been a better teacher than Jesus, and His characteristic mode of teaching was the parable (see Mark 4:33–34). The parables illustrated Jesus' kingdom message, making the ethereal understandable. But there is more to it than that. Parables do more than illustrate the message of Jesus; they are means of divine revelation.

In this chapter, we will consider the role that parables play in the kingdom of God. Through parables, Jesus taught us much about the nature of the kingdom. But He also used parables as part of His strategy to usher in the kingdom. We will consider what a parable is and look at the way that the parables teach us about the kingdom.

Just as there is a division between Jesus' kingdom and the kingdom of the devil, so there is a division between those who understand the parables of the kingdom and those who do not.

What Is a Parable?

Old Testament Precedents

To begin, we need to be clear about what a parable is. Parable can be difficult to define. They are sometimes thought of simply as illustrations—maybe earthly stories with a heavenly truth. While there is much truth to this, there is something even more profound about parables.

As with so much about the kingdom, we need to understand the Old Testament precedents for parables. One of the modes of speech for Old Testament prophets was designated by the Hebrew term *mashal*, something like a riddle or a proverb. For example, Solomon spoke three thousand proverbs, and the Hebrew word here is *mashal* (1 Kings 4:32; see also 1 Sam. 10:12; 24:13; Eccl. 12:9). If King Solomon was a speaker of parables (1 Kings 4:32), Jesus is more so. Parables were also a mode of speech known to the prophets (e.g., Ezek. 12:22–23; 17:2; 20:49; see also Ps. 78:2). To speak in parables, therefore, is to speak as a prophet.

Further, the prophets often communicated their messages by visible signs. The following are examples of this:

- Isaiah for a time walked around naked and barefoot.
- Jeremiah buried a waistcloth and the deed to a piece of land.

- Ezekiel lay on his left side for 390 days and his right side for 40 days.
- Hosea was instructed to marry a prostitute.

This is just a small sample. Such actions were visible words of the prophets, illustrating the nature of their messages. Therefore, these "sign acts" were like visible parables for the people. As we have seen, Jesus engaged in sign acts, most notably through His miracles that demonstrated the nature of the kingdom. Jesus illustrated the nature of the kingdom through the signs of miracles (see chapter 6 above), but our focus in this chapter is mainly on His verbal parabolic ministry.

As a teacher of parables, Jesus is the true King of a greater kingdom than Solomon. Jesus is also the long-awaited prophet like Moses (Deut. 18:15, 18). Indeed, as our Mediator, He is our King, our Prophet, and our Priest. All that these offices represent, Christ fulfills.

Defining a Parable

We still need to define in more detail what a parable is. On this question, there is a range of opinions. Sometimes parables are understood to be allegories, whereby each element of the parable is a cipher for something else. One often-discussed example is Augustine's interpretation of the parable of the good Samaritan (Luke 10:29–37), in which every element in the parable represents something else. For example, in Augustine's interpretation:[1]

---

1 Discussed in C.H. Dodd, *The Parables of the Kingdom* (Nisbet, 1935), 11–12.

- The man on his way from Jerusalem to Jericho is Adam.
- The thieves who attacked the man are the devil and demons.
- The priest and the Levite who passed by the other side represent the Old Testament.
- The Samaritan who helped the man is Christ.
- The innkeeper they meet later is the Apostle Paul.

As ingenious as this interpretation is—and as true as the theological framework may be—this approach fails to consider the parable sufficiently and accurately in its original context. The original audience would not have been able to understand this interpretation. To point to only one example, Jesus is not a Samaritan.

At the opposite end of the spectrum are those who deny that the parables are in any way allegorical. This is often associated with a historical-critical approach to the Gospels wherein we try to peel away layers of the parables to find the historical "core," and when we do that, the argument goes that anything that looks allegorical was added later and is not what Jesus really said. This approach is extremely problematic. As I discussed in chapter 1, it is not our job to adjudicate the true from the false in the Gospels; all parts of the Gospels are true. Further, this approach fails to account for the contexts of the parables in the flow of the gospel narratives, arguing—unpersuasively—that the contexts are secondary and are not necessary for the right interpretation of the Gospels.

The best approach lies between these two extremes. The parables are not primarily allegories whereby we can force their elements to serve as a code for something else. But it is equally mistaken to think that the parables cannot correlate to other details in the gospel narratives. For example, the account of the strong man and the stronger man we considered in the previous chapter communicates the victory of Jesus over the devil. It is noteworthy that Mark identifies this as a parable (Mark 3:23). Similarly, one of Jesus' final parables, the parable of the tenants addressed to the religious leadership during Passion Week (Mark 12:1–12), correlates to the impending death of Jesus at the hands of the religious leaders. The beloved son corresponds to Jesus, who is known elsewhere as God's beloved Son (see 1:11; 9:7), and the murderers represent the religious leadership, who have been plotting Jesus' death since the early chapters of Mark (see 3:6). Further emphasizing this contextual interpretation is the response of His opponents: They recognized that He spoke the parable against them (12:12).

To appreciate the way that these parables correlate to other portions in the Gospels requires us to read them in context. This is another reason that it's important to read the Gospels as continuous narratives and not as isolated episodes. The parables are part of the progressively revealed gospel in the Gospels.

At the same time, not every parable so strongly correlates to the events of the Gospels. To understand parables, we need a definition that is suitably flexible to include all manners of parables that we encounter in the Gospels.

One of the classic definitions comes from the first half of the twentieth century. New Testament scholar C.H. Dodd argued that a parable is "a metaphor or simile drawn from nature or common life, arresting the hearer by its vividness or strangeness, and leaving the mind in sufficient doubt about its precise application to tease it into active thought."[2] This definition is good, though I would nuance it a bit; a parable does not always leave the audience in sufficient doubt about its precise application.[3] Sometimes the application is clear. For example, at the conclusion of the parable of the good Samaritan in Luke 10:37, Jesus says, "You go, and do likewise."[4]

At the same time, it is indeed important to appreciate that parables are often vivid and strange. We do not understand the parables accurately if we simply make them obvious natural lessons that have spiritual truths. Often the spiritual truth is made from an incongruity in what we would expect.[5] What makes the parables memorable is often their unexpectedness. Parables make surprising points, which correlates to the surprising nature of the kingdom.

It is difficult to capture the complexity of parables with a simple definition. If I were to venture my own definition, building on Dodd's classic definition, I would say that parables in the Gospels are stories or illustrations from everyday life, often strange or surprising, that communicate the often surprising character of the transcendent kingdom of God (often in relation to Christ) and require faith to understand rightly.

The Kingdom Comes Through Parables

One of the key, paradigmatic parables is the parable of the sower. This parable depicts the importance of the Word of God in the

2 Dodd, *Parables of the Kingdom*, 16.

3 Klyne R. Snodgrass, *Stories with Intent: A Comprehensive Guide to the Parables of Jesus* (Eerdmans, 2008), 7.

4 Augustine also recognized this. See *On Christian Doctrine* 1.30.31.

5 See David Seccombe, "Incongruity in the Gospel Parables," *Tyndale Bulletin* 62 (2011): 161–72.

coming of the kingdom and gives Jesus occasion to discuss the purpose of parables. In what follows, I will consider this parable from its context in Mark 4:1–20. A sower sows seed in various places: some on the path, where it was eaten by birds; some on rocky ground, where it sprouted but soon withered; some among thorns, where it was choked; and some on good soil. Of these four sowings, only the fourth bore fruit. But the yield of this fruit was great: thirty-, sixty-, or a hundredfold.

We are not left to guess what this parable means because Jesus explains it later to His disciples (vv. 13–20). The seed is the Word of God. The seed that fell by the path was taken away by the devil. The seed that fell among rocky soil withered under the heat of persecution. The thorns represent the cares of this world and the deceitfulness of wealth. But the seed that fell on the good soil took root and produced an incredibly fruitful harvest.

This parable explains the relationship of the Word of God to the kingdom. Matthew refers to the seed as "the word of the kingdom" (Matt. 13:19). The parable of the sower reveals the close relationship between the preaching of the Word of God and the spread of the kingdom. This includes the preaching of parables, which is a means by which the kingdom will grow. Agricultural imagery, which would have been familiar to Jesus' audiences, was a common way for Jesus to explain the kingdom.

The Word of God is effectual; it gets results. Therefore, parables, as the Word of God, are effectual as well. Jesus explains the purpose of parables in Mark 4:10–12:

> And when he was alone, those around him with the twelve asked him about the parables. And he said to them, "To you has been

> given the secret of the kingdom of God, but for those outside everything is in parables, so that
>
> "'they may indeed see but not perceive,
> and may indeed hear but not understand,
> lest they should turn and be forgiven.'"

Like the Word of God more broadly, the parables of Jesus both conceal and reveal, depending on a person's faith commitment. On the one hand, to understand parables is to understand the kingdom; this understanding is a gift given by God. On the other hand, for those outside the kingdom, the parables remain hidden. In fact, Jesus' point is that parables are a means of the Word of God to harden the hearts of those who do not believe. This is a great mystery but refers both to God's divine purpose and to the responsibility each person has to believe rightly.

But for those to whom it has been given, parables reveal the mystery of the kingdom. The seed may itself be an Old Testament image. Isaiah prophesies of a coming day when the Word of God would accomplish its purpose:

> "For as the rain and the snow come down from heaven
> and do not return there but water the earth,
> making it bring forth and sprout,
> giving seed to the sower and bread to the eater,
> so shall my word be that goes out from my mouth;
> it shall not return to me empty,
> but it shall accomplish that which I purpose,
> and shall succeed in the thing for which I sent it.

"For you shall go out in joy
and be led forth in peace;
the mountains and the hills before you
shall break forth into singing,
and all the trees of the field shall clap their hands.
Instead of the thorn shall come up the cypress;
instead of the brier shall come up the myrtle;
and it shall make a name for the LORD,
an everlasting sign that shall not be cut off." (Isa. 55:10–13)

Isaiah is looking forward to a new work of redemption that will be accomplished among God's people through the powerful Word of God. God would reestablish His people by His Word, and the people would be regathered. God's Word would produce good fruit; the kingdom would be reestablished, and His people would reap the bounty.

Indeed, it is not to be missed that the parables are parables *of the kingdom*. The parables are largely about the kingdom, and therefore, they are a primary way we learn about it.

Exploring the Kingdom Through Parables

Jesus has much more to say about the kingdom through parables. If the parables are often surprising, so, too, is the kingdom. We cannot cover all of Jesus' parables, but it will be helpful to consider some of the ways that the parables reveal to us the nature of the kingdom, especially from Mark 4 and Matthew 13.

Mustard Seed

Jesus uses the analogy of a seed to discuss the kingdom in the parable of the mustard seed:

> And he said, "With what can we compare the kingdom of God, or what parable shall we use for it? It is like a grain of mustard seed, which, when sown on the ground, is the smallest of all the seeds on earth, yet when it is sown it grows up and becomes larger than all the garden plants and puts out large branches, so that the birds of the air can make nests in its shade." (Mark 4:30–32; see also Matt. 13:31–32)

Here Jesus compares the kingdom to something proverbially small (a mustard seed) that turns into the largest of all the trees. The basic point is that the kingdom starts small and apparently innocuously but grows into something so massively huge that it is a tree that provides shade for the whole world. In other words, the kingdom may not seem like a massive movement at first, but in the end it will be a kingdom that provides refuge for the nations.

But there is even more to the parable. Notice the contrast between the mustard seed and the tree: Though the mustard seed is the smallest of seeds, it turns into a tree so massively huge that all the birds of heaven can nest in its branches. This is surprising. It is not surprising that Jesus says that the mustard seed is the smallest of seeds. Some interpreters have been stumped on this point, since seeds that are smaller than the mustard seed exist. But that misses Jesus' point. He is not providing a science lesson; He is speaking proverbially. It was well known in the ancient world that a mustard seed represented something small.[6] Jesus is using that known proverb to make a new point. It is like someone's saying today, "A rolling stone gathers no moss." You would not disprove that proverb if you

6 See Snodgrass, *Stories with Intent*, 220, 662n200.

happened to find a stone falling down a cliff that had some moss on it. It's proverbial.

What is surprising is the size of the tree that results from the seed; it is big enough for all the birds of heaven to nest in its branches. Notice in the passage quoted above that the mustard seed "becomes larger than all the *garden plants*." Garden plants—that is, garden vegetables—don't have branches big enough for all the birds of heaven. In fact, the mustard seed in view does not normally grow into a massive tree and does not normally have branches big enough for all the birds of the air.[7] The point is not to try to defend this parable botanically, as though all that Jesus meant were that sometimes the mustard plant grows big enough for small birds to rest. Instead, Jesus' point is that the kingdom of God is like the smallest of seeds that becomes much larger than one would expect. The incongruity makes it memorable. For us to appreciate the force of this parable requires a bit of historical legwork.

Further, as with so much of Jesus' teaching, to gain the fullest effect we must give attention to the Old Testament background. In this case, two Old Testament passages stand out.[8] One comes from Daniel, which we saw has much to say about the future kingdom of God. In Daniel 4, Nebuchadnezzar's kingdom is compared to a massive tree that provides shade and food for all the birds of the heavens (vv. 10–12). In this case, the tree was cut down, which represented humbling Nebuchadnezzar and his becoming like an animal. Nebuchadnezzar's kingdom was tremendously successful, but it was temporary. Even so, it anticipates a fuller, worldwide kingdom that will never end—the kingdom of God.

---

7 Seccombe, "Incongruity in the Gospel Parables," 162–64.

8 Seccombe, "Incongruity in the Gospel Parables," 163–64.

A second Old Testament text comes from a parable in Ezekiel 17. This parable speaks about the Babylonians, who attacked and subdued Jerusalem (vv. 11–15). The king of Jerusalem will be cast off by the Lord and the people scattered (vv. 19–21). But in the future, the Lord would plant a sprig from a cedar of Lebanon, and when it was planted it would become a great cedar tree, and in its branches all sorts of birds would find shade (vv. 3–4, 22–24). This "sprig" speaks of the coming Messiah and the flourishing of His future kingdom.[9]

This Old Testament background provides precedents for the parable of the mustard seed. Though the kingdom starts out small and innocuously, in the end it will become a massive, worldwide kingdom.

Hidden Leaven

The parable of the leaven is like the parable of the mustard seed. It is only one verse long, but it shows the spread of the kingdom: "He told them another parable. 'The kingdom of heaven is like leaven that a woman took and hid in three measures of flour, till it was all leavened'" (Matt. 13:33). To interpret this parable, we need to know how much three measures of flour is: This was around fifty pounds of flour (see Christian Standard Bible). That's a lot of flour! We are not sure why the woman would have so much flour, but when the hidden leaven expands in the flour, it would cause the fifty pounds of flour to expand and probably burst its container. The hidden leaven would not remain hidden but would make its presence known.[10] It's like

9 See Daniel I. Block, *The Book of Ezekiel*, New International Commentary on the Old Testament (Eerdmans, 1997), 1:550–52.

10 Here I have been helped by Seccombe, "Incongruity in the Gospel Parables," 167–70.

pouring a whole bottle of soap into a bubble bath. It will expand and overflow the tub.

I'm reminded of a leaky tire I once had on my car. The sensor in my tire told me that I was losing air, but it was impossible to see the leak with the naked eye. I kicked my tire and examined it, but it seemed like it was full of air. Nevertheless, I dutifully drove to an air pump and attached it to an air hose, and sure enough, the tire needed air. I could not tell by looking that my tire was leaking air, but given enough time, it would have been completely flat. Then it would have been impossible to miss.

This is a negative example, but the point is like the parable of the leaven. We may not be able to see the kingdom now. It is often hidden in this age. But it will continue to spread and grow by God's power. In the end, its presence will be impossible to miss, and it will be expansive and grand in scale.

Hidden Treasure

Keeping with the "hidden" theme, Jesus also compares the kingdom to a treasure hidden in a field and a pearl of great value (Matt. 13:44–46). When we discover this treasure, we should recognize it for the supreme value that it is. The kingdom is more precious than anything else we can acquire, and we ought to do all we can to enter that kingdom.

Parables of a Gracious Kingdom

We have by no means looked at all the aspects of the kingdom communicated through parables, but I hope to have provided a taste for how kingdom-oriented the parables are and how they teach us about the nature of the kingdom. The kingdom starts small but will continue to grow in this age, ultimately becoming worldwide in scope. The parables often teach us what it means to respond appropriately to the kingdom.

Since the kingdom is so valuable, we ought to do all that we can to enter it. We are to seek the kingdom (Luke 12:31). At the same time, the kingdom is not something that we can earn or make by our own efforts.[11] It is God who grants us the kingdom (12:32).[12] We are not worthy to enter the kingdom, but we are to receive it like a small child (18:17). Small children are dependent on others for all that they receive, and we enter the kingdom not through our own good works or through worldly wealth (see 18:18–30) but through the mediatorial work of Christ.

11 Vos, *Teaching of Jesus*, 47.

12 Ridderbos, *Coming of the Kingdom*, 76.

Practical Takeaways

1. The kingdom of God is closely related to the Word of God. Let us ensure that the Word finds good soil in our hearts and takes root that we may bear fruit.
2. The kingdom of God starts small and inconspicuously in this age, but it will grow into a worldwide, everlasting kingdom. It may not seem like much now, and the world may not recognize it, but what starts small will grow and grow until the consummation.
3. The kingdom is granted to us as a gift. In the kingdom, the first will be last and the last will be first. We are to seek the kingdom but also recognize that the kingdom is granted to us as a gift (Luke 12:31–32).[13]

13 I don't recall if this is my point or if I gleaned it from someone along the way; cf. Vos, *Teaching of Jesus*, 12, 70.

9

The Ethics of the Kingdom

If you've ever traveled to another country—or even to other parts of the same country—you may have recognized different customs and ways of doing things. One common difference is food, which is often distinctive to particular areas. You may notice other differences such as clothing, dialects, and social conventions.

Our actions and the way that we "do life" may vary in the details depending on where we live. At the same time, if you happen to be a transplant from one region to another, you may retain some of your native customs even in a new culture. You may speak a different language at home than you do in public. You may choose to eat foods that reflect where you're from, and you may retain values that were instilled in you as important, even if those around you do not hold to quite the same customs.

If we believe in Christ and participate in the kingdom of God, we have a new citizenship. Though we live in this present evil age, our lives are guided by a heavenly reality. We are citizens of the kingdom of righteousness, and our lives should reflect that righteousness. Though we do not earn our way into the kingdom of God, we are called to reflect the priorities of the kingdom in our daily life—even as those priorities may differ from the world around us.

Thankfully, Jesus has much to say about how we are to live in the kingdom of God. But sometimes Jesus' words have been misunderstood. This chapter will look mostly at one of the most famous sections of the Gospels in which Jesus addresses how we are to live in the kingdom: the Sermon on the Mount in Matthew 5–7. The Sermon on the Mount is not an abstract code of conduct; it is specifically about how to live as disciples in the kingdom of God. We will look at the context for the Sermon on the Mount and how it helps us understand what our lives are to look like as members of the kingdom of God.

Kingdom Context

Some well-known sayings and Bible verses come from the Sermon on the Mount:

> "Judge not, that you be not judged." (Matt. 7:1)
> "Turn the other cheek." (see 5:39)
> "Our Father which art in heaven." (6:9, KJV)
> "Blessed are the peacemakers." (5:9)
> "Blessed are the meek." (5:5)
> "Don't cast your pearls before swine." (see 7:6)

You may think of other portions of the Sermon on the Mount that could be added to this list. Some of these statements may be familiar even to those who don't know much about Scripture. Yet how often do people consider the wider context of the Sermon on the Mount when they invoke these statements? The context of these statements must be duly appreciated.

Put simply, to understand the Sermon on the Mount requires us to read it in its proper context. The Sermon on the Mount is not simply advice for anyone who would dip in and use it to become a better person irrespective of their commitment to Jesus. No, the Sermon on the Mount must be read in the context of the Gospel of Matthew, the larger context of the New Testament, and all Scripture. More specifically, the ministry of Jesus provides the context for the Sermon on the Mount. Jesus did not come simply to propound abstract moral truth. Instead, He came to save His people from their sins (1:21), calling them to life in a new kingdom.

In Matthew's gospel, Jesus did not begin His ministry with the Sermon on the Mount. Instead, He first was baptized, overcame temptation, preached the gospel, and called disciples before He ever preached the Sermon on the Mount. Jesus' work takes center stage in the Gospels, and the Sermon on the Mount must be understood in that context. It is significant that the Sermon on the Mount is addressed to the disciples whom Jesus has called, who respond positively to the kingdom message (4:17–22; 5:1).

The Sermon on the Mount is meant especially for disciples of Jesus. While it is true that all people are required to obey their Creator, it is helpful to appreciate that the Sermon on the Mount shows us what it looks like to live as citizens of the kingdom of heaven following the pattern of Christ. Indeed, the righteousness that He teaches is the righteousness that He embodies. To understand the Sermon on the Mount is to see it through the eyes of faith with the commitment of discipleship.

To understand the Sermon on the Mount, let's consider its context. Quite significant for that context is the kingdom emphasis of Matthew's gospel. Notice the following details drawn from the context of the Sermon on the Mount and the sermon itself, all of which mention the kingdom:

- Jesus' initial message in Matthew 4:17 is, "Repent, for the kingdom of heaven is at hand." This prepares us for His fuller teaching in Matthew 5–7.
- The first statement of blessing (or beatitude) in the Sermon on the Mount focuses on the kingdom of heaven (5:3).
- The final, short beatitude also focuses on the kingdom of heaven (v. 10), which forms a literary frame with the first beatitude. Both emphasize the present reality of the kingdom of heaven.
- Jesus emphasizes the importance of the "least of these commandments" for status in the kingdom of heaven and the need to have a greater righteousness than the scribes and Pharisees (vv. 19–20).
- In the Lord's Prayer, we pray for the kingdom to come (6:10).
- We are to seek first God's kingdom and His righteousness (v. 33).
- Jesus ends the Sermon on the Mount by addressing those who do and do not enter the kingdom of heaven (7:21–27).

These examples illustrate that the Sermon on the Mount describes to a significant degree the kingdom of heaven. To understand the sermon, therefore, requires us to appreciate the importance of its kingdom context.

Understanding the sermon also requires us to understand the phrase "kingdom *of heaven*." This is the phrase used in the Sermon on the Mount, and it is often used in the Gospel of Matthew, whereas other Gospels typically employ the phrase "kingdom of God." Why does Matthew prefer "kingdom of heaven"? It has often been suggested that it is because Matthew is displaying reverence for the divine name and is hesitant to overuse the name of God.[1] While this is possible, it does not account for Matthew's willingness to use the divine name in many places elsewhere in the gospel, nor does it account for the use of both the phrases "kingdom of heaven" and "kingdom of God" in Matthew (see 6:33; 12:28; 19:24; 21:31, 43).

In recent years, scholars have revisited this question and argued (persuasively, in my opinion) that "kingdom of heaven" refers to the transcendence of God's kingdom in contrast to the sinfulness of our world. The "kingdom of heaven" alludes to the righteousness that is characteristic of heaven—God's abode—that should increasingly characterize our world as the kingdom takes root and spreads.[2] Put simply, "kingdom of heaven" refers to the heavenly righteousness that characterizes the kingdom of God, bringing with it the call for us to live righteously "on earth as it is in heaven" (6:10). So while

1 So Ridderbos, *Coming of the Kingdom*, 19.

2 See Thomas R. Schreiner, *New Testament Theology: Magnifying God in Christ* (Baker Academic, 2008), 45–47, summarizing Jonathan T. Pennington, *Heaven and Earth in the Gospel of Matthew*, Supplements to Novum Testamentum 126 (Brill, 2007).

"kingdom of God" and "kingdom of heaven" ultimately refer to the same reality, "kingdom *of heaven*" brings out the nuance of righteousness that characterizes the kingdom of God.

One of the best places in Matthew—and indeed in all the Gospels—where we see what the righteousness of the kingdom is to look like in practice is in the Sermon on the Mount.

Kingdom Message of the Sermon on the Mount

A Greater Righteousness

Now that we've seen the kingdom context for the Sermon on the Mount, we need to give more attention to its kingdom message. This consideration leads us to one of the perennial questions about the Sermon on the Mount: Does the Sermon present us with an unattainable ideal, or are we expected to be able to obey its teachings? One of the key passages here is Matthew 5:20: "For I tell you, unless your righteousness exceeds that of the scribes and Pharisees, you will never enter the kingdom of heaven." It is commonly thought that the scribes and Pharisees were extremely careful to obey the law of God, and no one today can really expect to outdo them when it comes to the righteousness that God requires. How, then, could we ever outdo them in righteousness?

But this view is mistaken. Jesus does not critique the scribes and Pharisees for paying *too much* attention to the law of God; rather, He critiques them for paying *too little* attention to the law of God. They followed their own man-made laws more assiduously than they followed God's law (see 15:1–9). They fixated on the small things and neglected the major things, as Jesus points out: "Woe to you, scribes and Pharisees, hypocrites! For you tithe mint and dill and cumin, and have neglected the weightier matters of the law: justice and mercy and faithfulness. These you ought to have done, without neglecting the others" (23:23). The greater righteousness Jesus requires of His disciples in Matthew 5:20 is not a hypothetical requirement or a statement to drive us to despair because we are not able to follow the law of God. Instead, Jesus really wants us to pay attention to God's law and live integrated, whole lives that are not hypocritical. In this way, our righteousness will exceed that of the scribes and Pharisees. Jesus wants us to emphasize the main points of the law, which He clarifies as love for God and love for neighbor—for on these two commandments hang all the Law and the Prophets (22:37–39).

Therefore, the term "righteousness" in the Sermon on the Mount refers to the obedience that the disciples of Jesus are required to pursue. The Sermon on the Mount provides primarily what Reformed theology often describes as the third use of the law: God's law is a guide for righteous living. This is true even in the New Testament, and this is true even though we cannot keep the law of God perfectly. What, then, is the Sermon on the Mount? Sinclair Ferguson's book title captures it well: It describes "kingdom life in a fallen world."[3]

In the Sermon on the Mount, Jesus provides a sketch for what it looks like to live as kingdom citizens in an ungodly world. Ridderbos argues that *righteousness* and *kingdom* "are synonymous concepts in Jesus' preaching."[4] The lifestyle of disciples is to be marked by greater and greater conformity to the law of God—greater and greater

---

3 Sinclair B. Ferguson, *The Sermon on the Mount: Kingdom Life in a Fallen World* (Banner of Truth, 1987).

4 Ridderbos, *Coming of the Kingdom*, 286.

holiness amid sinful society. By so doing, the people of the kingdom are like a city on a hill (5:14–16). The call is for kingdom people to be so concerned with holiness that they pay attention to how all of God's commandments relate to them in the kingdom era. The context preceding Matthew 5:20 is quite instructive in this:

> "Do not think that I have come to abolish the Law or the Prophets; I have not come to abolish them but to fulfill them. For truly, I say to you, until heaven and earth pass away, not an iota, not a dot, will pass from the Law until all is accomplished. Therefore whoever relaxes one of the least of these commandments and teaches others to do the same will be called least in the kingdom of heaven, but whoever does them and teaches them will be called great in the kingdom of heaven." (vv. 17–19)

Notice in verse 19 that to relax even one of the least of God's commandments leads to a lower standing in the kingdom of God, for life in the kingdom is to be marked by meticulous concern for how the law applies to life. Life in the kingdom is to be marked by holiness.

Notice the relation of our obedience to the law to Christ. This call to holiness is also the call to follow the pattern of Christ (see vv. 17–18). His earthly life was characterized by conformity to God's law. The righteousness that we are called to in practice assumes the righteousness that Jesus fulfills on our behalf (cf. 3:15). While we cannot obey the law of God perfectly in this age, we are called to obey the law in fellowship with Christ.

So while the Sermon on the Mount does indeed call us to practical obedience to the law of God, it does not do so in abstraction from the Savior, who fulfills all righteousness. Indeed, part of what it must mean to embody a greater righteousness than that of the scribes and Pharisees is to look to Christ as the truly righteous One. Not only did the scribes and Pharisees miss the nature of the righteous conformity to God's law that God requires, but they also missed the way that the Law and Prophets point forward to Christ—the perfectly righteous Savior.

This is another way of saying that before we understand the kingdom imperatives of the Sermon on the Mount, we need to contextualize it in the context of what Jesus does. The kingdom message of the Sermon on the Mount is to seek greater and greater righteousness—for, indeed, the kingdom is characterized by righteousness (see 6:33). The kingdom life is marked by righteousness in practice. This means that if we want to be kingdom-minded people, we need to be concerned with practical holiness, as we will see in the following discussion.

The Righteousness of the Redeemed

One of the ways that we see the Sermon on the Mount's application for kingdom citizens is in the opening beatitudes, which feature the language, "Blessed are . . ." (5:3–12). The Old Testament background for this blessing is significant. Part of the background surely comes from the blessed person of Psalm 1, who meditates on and walks according to the law of the Lord. But according to Charles L. Quarles,[5] another aspect of its background may come from Deuteronomy 33:29:

---

5 Charles L. Quarles, *Sermon on the Mount: Restoring Christ's Message to the Modern Church*, NAC Studies in Bible and Theology 11 (Broadman & Holman, 2011), 39.

> "Happy are you, O Israel! Who is like you,
> a people saved by the LORD,
> the shield of your help,
> and the sword of your triumph!"

The term translated "happy" in Hebrew is the same term as "blessed" in Psalm 1, and the Greek translation of Deuteronomy 33:29 uses the same word for "blessed" that is used in the Beatitudes. In Deuteronomy 33, the ones who are blessed are those redeemed by the Lord. The blessings of the Beatitudes and the paradigm of discipleship in the Sermon on the Mount have application to citizens of the kingdom—those who are redeemed by the Lord.

This background of redemption also correlates to the first beatitude: "Blessed are the poor in spirit, for theirs is the kingdom of heaven" (Matt. 5:3). Here we need to linger over the category "poor in spirit," which in Luke's version simply reads, "Blessed are you who are poor" (Luke 6:20). Who are the poor in the Beatitudes? To answer this requires us again to consider the kingdom context for the Sermon on the Mount. We saw earlier that the gospel is described as good news for the poor (Luke 4:18), and Jesus draws attention to His preaching to the poor as an indication that the kingdom had truly come (Matt. 11:5). Who are these poor?

Briefly stated, "the poor" collectively represent the redeemed of the Lord. The term "the poor," which Matthew clarifies means "poor in spirit," is a way to refer to the faithful remnant among God's people.[6] It refers to those who recognize their need for the Lord's intervention in their lives. "Poor" can be a summary, representative

---

6 See Ridderbos, *Coming of the Kingdom*, 187–92.

way for the Bible to refer to those who look away from themselves and to God's provision for help (see Pss. 9:18; 72:12). The poor do not trust in riches but in God for their consolation. In fact, even David can refer to himself in the Psalms as a poor man to indicate his reliance on God (e.g., Pss. 34:6; 40:17; 70:5; 86:1; 109:22). Additionally, in the first century, those who were faithful were often socially and economically marginalized. The poor do not look to this world for security but to God. The Beatitudes describe the blessings of the redeemed, even as they encourage us toward greater conformity to God's law.

Another portion of the Sermon on the Mount that clarifies the righteousness of the redeemed comes in Matthew 5:21–48. This section is often called "the antitheses," because Jesus contrasts His commands with what the people had heard. Crucially, Jesus is not contrasting His teaching with the law of God but with popular but misguided teaching about the law of God. Jesus is correcting bad teaching. In this section, Jesus clarifies what the greater righteousness looks like and what attention to "the least of these commandments" looks like. Among these six examples, at least four of them come from the Ten Commandments, as Jesus shows us what their application should look like among God's people.

For example, Jesus says that not only must we not murder, but we must not even have a hateful thought (Matt. 5:21–26; cf. the sixth commandment, "You shall not murder"). Not only must we not commit the physical act of adultery, but we must have pure thoughts (Matt. 5:27–30; cf. the seventh commandment, "You shall not commit adultery"). The holiness here is to be greater than only external; it is to be internal as well. This is a call away from hypocrisy and toward the integrated pursuit of the whole person toward holiness.

Here again the kingdom context clarifies what is in view. Jesus is not telling people how to make themselves worthy to enter the kingdom. We enter by grace as we turn from sin and turn to Christ. Instead, Jesus is showing us what the ideal righteousness of the kingdom is: integrated, true holiness. The call is not to the bare minimum of external holiness but to greater and greater holiness as we apply God's law in practice.

This is the call for kingdom citizens and why, if we want to be kingdom-minded, we must be integrated, holy people. Kingdom-mindedness should never be so abstract that it leaves behind our personal holiness.

As we conclude, it is helpful to note the way the Sermon on the Mount concludes: with the contrast between the foolish man who built his house on the sand and the wise man who built his house on the rock (Matt. 7:24–27). This may be a familiar illustration, but what may be less familiar is the application Jesus gives it. It is striking that Jesus does not say the one who built his house on the rock is the one who *believed* rightly. Instead, the one who built his house on the rock is the one who *put into practice* what Jesus said. If we are wise, we will seek to obey the Sermon on the Mount as we follow Christ. This is the kingdom call.

Practical Takeaways

1. Kingdom citizens should live in accord with the priorities of the kingdom, which Jesus makes known to us in the Sermon on the Mount (among other texts). To be *kingdom-minded* means we should be assiduously committed to the moral law of God.
2. We must beware of the danger of hypocrisy, of being divided between internal and external actions. James calls this being "double-minded" (James 1:8; 4:8). We are to be integrated and complete people, loving God with all our heart, soul, mind, and strength and loving our neighbor as ourselves. For indeed, all the Law and the Prophets hang on these commands (Matt. 22:37–38).

10

The Reversal of Worldly Standards

In the 2022 Kentucky Derby, a horse was added late to the race, barely making the deadline to enter, because another horse dropped out. His name was Rich Strike, and he was the least-favored horse in the race and one of the least-favored horses in any Kentucky Derby. If you watched the first half of the race, you probably wouldn't have noticed this horse. Twenty seconds in, he was in last place, with nineteen horses ahead of him.

But then something happened. Rich Strike came out of nowhere and started gaining ground. He made a move up the middle. He moved up along the inside rail. And as the horses came down the homestretch, Rich Strike was in an all-out sprint, charging after the leaders. When they crossed the finish line, it was the unexpected Rich Strike who had won the prestigious Kentucky Derby—a horse that wasn't even expected to run in the race at all. Before the race, very few people would have expected much from Rich Strike, but in hindsight we know he won. This is a great underdog story.

In a similar respect, the history of the kingdom of God is something like an underdog story. Israel's God is the true God over the whole world, and yet Israel often seemed like a small, insignificant people in the grand scheme of things. They started humbly with one family (of Abraham), and though they grew to be a great people, they eventually became enslaved to the powerful Egyptians. Yet the God of Israel continually and patiently fought for His people, establishing them in their land and giving them a king, with David as the model.

In this chapter, we will look at the way that the kingdom of God reverses worldly expectations. Like an underdog, the kingdom may look weak and inconsequential in this world, but those who are last will be first and those who are first will be last. We have already seen this in the teaching about the kingdom in the parables and the Sermon on the Mount. We will look in greater detail at what the Gospels say about the dynamics of the kingdom: The kingdom subverts worldly expectations, and the citizens of the kingdom who seem to be the underdogs in this age will in the end be exalted because they follow and trust the King of all kings, whose kingdom comes out on top in the end.

Reversal in the Beatitudes

Returning to the Sermon on the Mount, which we considered in the previous chapter, gives us the opportunity to consider what can be called the *ethics of reversal* in the kingdom of God. *Ethics* simply refers to how we live. The kingdom of God does not operate according to worldly standards or priorities. It does not reward the rich and powerful, but the poor and marginalized are favored. This is not because of an abstract economic reality; poverty profits a person nothing spiritually. Instead, the blessings of the kingdom come to those who by faith participate in the kingdom of God.

We can trace this line of thinking through other beatitudes. We do not often think of the meek and humble as those who are favored, but Jesus says that the meek will inherit the earth (Matt. 5:5). In this age, it often seems that those who prevail are the selfish, ambitious, and ruthless ones who claw their way to the top. But in the kingdom, those who are meek, who recognize their humility before God and others, will be honored with the covenantal blessings of God.

Likewise, the merciful will receive mercy (Matt. 5:7). To be "merciful" is to be kind and to show favor even when the other person does not deserve it. Though this may seem like a tall order, Jesus reminds us that the mercy that we show to others correlates to the mercy that we want to receive from God (cf. James 2:13). Our call again is not to be ruthless and self-centered but to be compassionate and considerate to those around us (cf. Luke 10:37).

In our world, it is often not the peacemakers who are honored (see Matt. 5:9); those who are violent and bombastic become famous and receive accolades. But the kingdom of God is different. Our King is the Prince of Peace (Isa. 9:6), and those who follow in and implement the peace characteristics of our King will be called "sons of God" (Matt. 5:9) and will therefore receive an everlasting inheritance.

Indeed, in the kingdom those who are persecuted for righteousness are not scoffed at, ridiculed, or trampled on. Instead, those in the kingdom who are persecuted are *blessed* (Matt. 5:10–12), which also runs contrary to the spirit of this age, where those who are persecuted are marginalized and left behind. But as Jesus explains in more detail elsewhere, such people are blessed in the kingdom. This also characterizes our Savior, who suffered for us, even to the point of giving up His own life that He may be exalted on the other side.

Reversal in Mary's Song

Mary, the mother of Jesus, speaks about the reversal of worldly expectations in her famous Magnificat in Luke 1:46–55, in which she reflects on the great salvation that God is bringing through the child that she is bearing:

> And Mary said,
>
> "My soul magnifies the Lord,
> and my spirit rejoices in God my Savior. . . .
> He has shown strength with his arm;
> he has scattered the proud in the thoughts of
> their hearts;
> he has brought down the mighty from their thrones
> and exalted those of humble estate;
> he has filled the hungry with good things,
> and the rich he has sent away empty."
> (vv. 46–47, 51–53)

Mary reflects on what we saw in the previous chapter: that the poor in spirit are blessed in the kingdom (see Matt. 5:3). The poor look to the Lord for their help, and since they do so, they are blessed. Notice the contrast in Mary's song between the proud in their hearts and those of humble estate. Those who are proud and mighty in this age—those who are not poor in spirit, who do not look to the Lord for their help—are going to be brought low through the work of God in behalf of those who look to Him. Those who are rich and privileged in this age will be sent away empty, and those who look to the Lord for their sustenance will be rewarded.

Mary's song is not about abstract economic principles. It is a song about the coming of Christ, the true King, who would reign over the house of Jacob forever (Luke 1:31–33). When His kingdom comes, He reverses worldly expectations: Those who are favored and exalted are the lowly, and those who are proud and mighty will be brought low. The kingdom of God does not simply reinforce the power structures of this age; the kingdom of God instead brings a drastically different ethos of life.

This principle is expounded further in the epistle of James: "But the humble brother must boast in his high position, and the wealthy [brother] in his humiliation" (James 1:9–10, author's translation). James teaches the church what it looks like to live according to the standards of the kingdom of God. Those who are humble can boast—in the Lord—because in the kingdom the humble are exalted. In fact, it is the poor who are chosen to be heirs of the kingdom that God promises to those who love Him (James 2:5). Likewise, the wealthy brother can boast in his humiliation, which refers to the fleetingness of his earthly wealth.

This also helps us understand again that the kingdom is not about abstract principles. It is big enough to include both the rich and the poor. No one is automatically in the kingdom because they are poor, and no one is automatically out because they are rich. Instead, what matters is faith in Christ; we recognize that the power structures of this age are relative because wealth will not last forever, but neither will poverty.

The Last Will Be First

To these texts many others could be added that show the reversal of worldly status in the kingdom, including Mark 9:33–37:

> And they came to Capernaum. And when he was in the house he asked them, "What were you discussing on the way?" But they kept silent, for on the way they had argued with one another about who was the greatest. And he sat down and called the twelve. And he said to them, "If anyone would be first, he must be last of all and servant of all." And he took a child and put him in the midst of them, and taking him in his arms, he said to them, "Whoever receives one such child in my name receives me, and whoever receives me, receives not me but him who sent me."

In this context, Jesus is on His way to suffer and die in Jerusalem, and He is explaining to His disciples the nature of His messiahship. Three times He predicts His death and resurrection, and three times He clarifies the meaning of discipleship.

The disciples' understanding of greatness at this point was still shaped by worldly expectations. They were seeking to import worldly status and rank into the kingdom. But Jesus corrects them and explains that the kingdom of God does not work that way.

Instead, greatness in the kingdom is to become like a child. A small child is entirely dependent on others. Further, children are not often impressed by worldly status. I remember when I was young and attended a celebrity golf tournament in my hometown. I may have recognized a few famous people, but most of the famous people had to be pointed out to me. To a child, celebrities and local residents looked the same. I had my picture taken with a famous singer, but someone had to tell me that the person was a famous singer. I was just a child, and I didn't know this was a person I should have been impressed with.

To be great in the kingdom is to be like a child and is not to live according to worldly standards. In fact, Jesus tells us that we must receive the kingdom as a child (Luke 18:17). As we saw earlier, the kingdom of God is a gracious kingdom.

Further, to be great in the kingdom means to be a servant. This follows the pattern of Christ, who, as we will see, served to the point of laying down His life for His disciples. To be a servant of all is not something that the world views as great—such people are often overlooked or viewed as unimportant in the eyes of the world. But that is not the way that the kingdom of God operates.

Other statements Jesus makes reflect these principles:

> "But many who are first will be last, and the last first." (Mark 10:31)
> "For everyone who exalts himself will be humbled, and he who humbles himself will be exalted." (Luke 14:11)

These statements are true about the kingdom of God, and they also reflect the character of the King of the kingdom. The kingdom does not play by worldly rules; it reflects a different set of priorities altogether.

Practical Takeaways

1. The priorities of the kingdom of God do not reflect the priorities of this world. Worldly status profits a person nothing in the kingdom. In the gospel, God esteems

what is weak and foolish in the eyes of the world (1 Cor. 1:18–25). We therefore should not use worldly lenses to determine what (or who) is important in the kingdom of God. If God has chosen the poor to be rich in faith, then we ought to honor them as important in the kingdom and not show favoritism to the rich and powerful (see James 2:1–13).

2. Greatness in the kingdom is marked by service, not by self-promotion. Jesus tells us that the first will be last, and the last will be first. Kingdom citizens are to be marked by humility and sacrificial love, which follows the pattern of Christ.
3. The pattern of our lives in the kingdom is Christ—the One who emptied Himself for us, becoming obedient even unto death, that we may live through Him. The self-sacrificial love that Christ has shown us not only saves us from our sins but is a model for how we ought to interact with one another.

11

The People of the Kingdom

One of the silly rhymes that I learned as a child—maybe you know it, too—involved making a church shape with my hands, extending my index fingers to make a steeple, opening my hands to represent doors, wiggling my fingers to depict people, and reciting the following:

> Here is the church (hands together).
> Here is the steeple (forefingers raised).
> Open the door (palms turned up),
> and see all the people (wiggling fingers).

With a more theologically adept approach, we might change the words to reflect a stronger theology:

> Here is the *building* (hands together).
> Here is the steeple (forefingers raised).

Open the door (palms turned up),
and see *the church* (wiggling fingers).

The latter version is more theologically nuanced—the church is properly the people rather than the building—but it loses the cadence of the rhyme. To be fair, I don't know who originally wrote this ditty, but I doubt that its intent was to present a comprehensive theology of the church.

In this chapter, we will consider in more detail the makeup of the people of the kingdom. Where do they come from? How do they relate in the kingdom? If Jesus is the promised Son of David, how does His role as the King of Israel relate to the call for gentiles also to enter the kingdom? In brief, we will discuss the people of the kingdom, which is the church. In that light, we will also look at the debated question of the relationship between the kingdom of God and the church. Are they the same? Are they different? How should we understand the relationship between the kingdom and the church? This chapter is about the people of the kingdom.[1]

The True King of Israel

To understand the coming of the kingdom in the Gospels, we need to understand the historical background of Jesus' kingship. We have seen that the kingdom of God will eventually reach the whole world (see chapter 8), and I will discuss later how Jesus is indeed the King for the whole world. But before we talk about that, we need to address again how Jesus is the promised King of Israel. Before the blessings

1 On the importance of people for understanding the kingdom, see Patrick Schreiner, *Kingdom of God*, 18–19.

come to the nations, the kingdom of Israel must be restored, and the King must be reestablished on His throne.

We saw in chapter 2 the importance of the Davidic covenant for understanding the kingdom; the promise was given to David that one of his sons would reign over the kingdom of God forever. The Gospels narrate for us how Jesus is this promised Son of David and how He indeed reigns over the kingdom forever. A few snapshots from the Gospels illustrate the centrality of Israel in the ministry of Jesus.

Feeding Five Thousand

One way that we see this is in the feeding of the five thousand. As we saw earlier (in chapter 6 on miracles), Jesus' feeding the five thousand comes in the context of the true Davidic King's coming to shepherd His people (Matt. 9:36). Those who were fed in this case are most likely the sheep of Israel—that is, those of Jewish background. The twelve baskets of leftover food must in some way recall the twelve tribes of Israel, perhaps indicating the abundant provision of the true Shepherd for His people.

The Birth of Israel's King

The Gospels also speak in many other ways of Jesus as the true Davidic King who shepherds His people. One way comes from a familiar Christmas passage:

> And in the same region there were shepherds out in the field, keeping watch over their flock by night. And an angel of the Lord appeared to them, and the glory of the Lord shone around them, and they were filled with great fear. And the angel said to them,

> "Fear not, for behold, I bring you good news of great joy that will be for all the people. For unto you is born this day in the city of David a Savior, who is Christ the Lord. And this will be a sign for you: you will find a baby wrapped in swaddling cloths and lying in a manger." (Luke 2:8–12)

Notice especially the phrasing in Luke 2:10: "I bring you good news of great joy that will be for all *the* people." This is the translation of the ESV, but the older and perhaps more familiar version to some is the KJV, which reads, "I bring you good tidings of great joy, which shall be *to all people*." Notice the slight difference here between "all *the* people" (ESV) and the simple statement "to all people" (KJV). Perhaps it is natural to think that the angel simply means the good news of Jesus' birth is relevant for all people throughout the world. And that is indeed true, understood rightly. But why, then, does the ESV say "all *the* people"?

To understand this, it will be helpful to recall that Jesus comes in fulfillment of the Davidic covenant. "All the people" here is probably the better translation of the Greek text, since the context is specifically about Jesus' fulfilling the Davidic covenant. Notice what the angel says has happened in Luke 2:11: "For unto you is born this day in the city of David a Savior, who is Christ the Lord." Jesus' birth is in the city of David, fulfilling the prophecy of a coming Son of David who would be born in Bethlehem (Mic. 5:2). The term "Christ" refers specifically to the anointed Son of David, fulfilling texts such as Psalm 2:2. This is what it means for Him to be the Messiah.

"All *the* people," therefore, has a particular people in view: the people of Israel. The angel is telling the shepherds that their long-awaited King has been born. This is good news for all the people of

Israel. But this also means it is good news for the whole world, as we will see later in this chapter.

The Movement of Redemptive History

Since Jesus comes as the long-awaited King of Israel, the Gospels to a significant degree narrate the ministry of Christ among His own people. Most of Jesus' teaching, miraculous works, and dining happened among Jewish people. In the first century, the cultural and religious divisions between Jews and non-Jews were quite stark, and many of these barriers were still in effect during the ministry of Jesus. While Jesus did engage with gentiles (see next section), most of His ministry was focused on the people of Israel. The long-awaited King had come to shepherd His people, leading them in righteousness.

We see in Jesus' ministry what Paul will later describe as "to the Jew first" (see Rom. 1:16). One text that makes this clear is Jesus' instructions to His disciples before sending them out to minister: "These twelve Jesus sent out, instructing them, 'Go nowhere among the Gentiles and enter no town of the Samaritans, but go rather to the lost sheep of the house of Israel. And proclaim as you go, saying, "The kingdom of heaven is at hand"'" (Matt. 10:5–7).

It may seem odd to us these many centuries later that Jesus told His disciples *not* to travel among the gentiles but to go only to the lost sheep of the house of Israel. To understand this directive means that we must appreciate the initial stage of the kingdom's coming, which focuses on God's historic covenant people of Israel. Later, these same disciples will indeed minister to the nations. But at this early point in the coming of the kingdom—before the death and resurrection of Jesus—the focus is primarily on bringing good news to

Israel. Yet as we will see below, that good news for Israel is also good news for the nations.

The King for All People(s)

Old Testament Anticipations

As the promised Son of David, Jesus is also the King for all peoples. This is because the kingdom of God is to spread over all the earth, and the nations will come in submission to the Davidic King and pay homage to Him. This also was anticipated in the Old Testament. The following examples show this anticipation:

> Now therefore, O kings, be wise;
>   be warned, O rulers of the earth.
> Serve the LORD with fear,
>   and rejoice with trembling.
> Kiss the Son,
>   lest he be angry, and you perish in the way,
>   for his wrath is quickly kindled.
> Blessed are all who take refuge in him. (Ps. 2:10–12)

> It shall come to pass in the latter days
>   that the mountain of the house of the LORD
> shall be established as the highest of the mountains,
>   and shall be lifted up above the hills;
> and all the nations shall flow to it,
>   and many peoples shall come, and say:
> "Come, let us go up to the mountain of the LORD,
>   to the house of the God of Jacob,

that he may teach us his ways
  and that we may walk in his paths."
For out of Zion shall go forth the law,
  and the word of the LORD from Jerusalem. (Isa. 2:2–3)

Arise, shine, for your light has come,
  and the glory of the LORD has risen upon you.
For behold, darkness shall cover the earth,
  and thick darkness the peoples;
but the LORD will arise upon you,
  and his glory will be seen upon you.
And nations shall come to your light,
  and kings to the brightness of your rising. (Isa. 60:1–3)

"In that day I will raise up
  the booth of David that is fallen
and repair its breaches,
  and raise up its ruins
  and rebuild it as in the days of old,
that they may possess the remnant of Edom
  and all the nations who are called by my name,"
  declares the LORD who does this. (Amos 9:11–12)

We can also illustrate the importance of the nations in the context of the kingdom with several snapshots from the Gospels.

Feeding Four Thousand

Jesus fed five thousand people as the messianic Shepherd; He also fed four thousand on another occasion. To understand why the Gospels recount two similar feeding episodes, it is helpful to observe that this latter feeding of four thousand occurs in a different context—most likely in the gentile area known as the Decapolis (see Mark 7:31). Here again we are reminded that we must read the Gospels not as a collection of isolated stories but as progressively unveiled integrated narratives. Just as the twelve baskets of food left over when Jesus fed the five thousand were significant, so the seven baskets of food left over after feeding the four thousand likely demonstrate the ample provision of the Jewish Messiah for all people.

A Light for the Gentiles

I noted earlier that "all *the* people" in Luke 2:10 most likely refers to all the people of Israel. Yet the good news of Jesus' birth is also for all people more broadly. This comes into clearer view with the Song of Simeon in Luke 2:

> "Lord, now you are letting your servant depart in peace,
> according to your word;
> for my eyes have seen your salvation
> that you have prepared in the presence of all peoples,
> a light for revelation to the Gentiles,
> and for glory to your people Israel." (vv. 29–32)

Simeon identifies the salvation that Jesus brings to be a light for the gentiles as well as for the glory of Israel. Jesus' birth is not good news *either* for Israel *or* for the gentiles; Jesus' birth is good news for both Israel and the gentiles.

As the narrative of Luke progresses, much of the emphasis is on the people of Israel (though with plenty of indication that Jesus' kingship is also for the nations), whereas the spread of the gospel to the nations more fully comes in the book of Acts after the resurrection and ascension of Jesus. Indeed, the book of Acts is largely about the kingdom's spreading from Israel to the nations as Jesus reigns from heaven over the whole world. Before the good news comes in fullness to the gentiles, the Gospels narrate how Jesus is restoring the kingship and the kingdom to Israel. This is the foundational assumption for the spread of the good news to the gentiles as well. In this light, the book of Acts has much to say about the kingdom of God—how Jesus is installed as the King at God's right hand and how the blessings of His worldwide kingship expand to all the nations (see Acts 1:8; 2:36).

Gentiles and True Faith

What is important for being a citizen of the kingdom of God is not physical heritage but faith in the promises of God. John the Baptist made it clear that the natural children of Abraham were not guaranteed God's blessing just because of their genealogy, for God could raise up children of Abraham from the stones if He desired (Matt. 3:7–9). What matters is true faith that bears the fruit of repentance. In fact, sometimes in the Gospels we find that gentiles—those who come from outside the kingdom of Israel—have greater faith than those who descend physically from Abraham.

Matthew makes it clear that Jesus' own family tree—that is, His royal genealogy—includes several faithful gentiles. Four gentiles are mentioned in Matthew's genealogy of Jesus: Tamar (1:3), Rahab (v. 5), Ruth (v. 5), and Uriah the Hittite (v. 6). Bathsheba's name is not given; instead, Uriah's name, a gentile name, is given. All four of these gentiles demonstrated great faith in the promises of God (though note that Uriah was not actually an ancestor of Jesus).

Tamar was more concerned with continuing the promised line of Abraham than her father-in-law, Judah (see Gen. 38:26). Rahab demonstrated true faith by harboring the Israelite spies and putting her trust in the God of Israel instead of in the gods of Jericho (Josh. 2:4–14; see also James 2:25). Ruth refused to leave her mother-in-law, Naomi, but committed herself to Israel's God and became the great-grandmother of King David (Ruth 1:16–17; 4:16–17). Uriah, the husband of Bathsheba, was one of David's most loyal and capable men and refused to enjoy a night of luxury with his wife while his men were fighting the Lord's battles (2 Sam. 11).

Elsewhere, Matthew notes the faith of a centurion who recognized his own unworthiness and Jesus' ability to heal the man's ailing servant from a distance. As a soldier with authority, the centurion recognized that when he gave a command, it would be followed; all Jesus had to do was command, and it would be done. Jesus then praises the man's faith:

> When Jesus heard this, he marveled and said to those who followed him, "Truly, I tell you, with no one in Israel have I found such faith. I tell you, many will come from east and west and recline at table with Abraham, Isaac, and Jacob in the kingdom of heaven, while the sons of the kingdom will be thrown into the outer darkness. In that place there will be weeping and gnashing of teeth." (8:10–12)

This centurion's faith was exemplary, even more than what Jesus had found in Israel. Those "from east and west" who will recline with the patriarchs in the kingdom of heaven refer to gentiles from outside the borders of Israel who, because of their faith, will participate in the consummate kingdom when Christ returns.

What matters for citizenship in the kingdom is not people's natural birthright but their faith. No one is guaranteed citizenship in the kingdom because of physical lineage; what matters is faith in the promises of God, particularly as they find their fulfillment in Christ.

To this we could add many other examples. In the context of Jesus' feeding the four thousand in Mark, Jesus critiques the hypocrisy of the Pharisees for honoring God with their lips and not their hearts and for elevating human commandments as though they were divine commandments (Mark 7:1–13). In contrast, He praises the faith of the gentile woman from Syrophoenicia who was satisfied merely with the crumbs of blessing that come from the Jewish Messiah. She knew that Jesus had the spiritual authority to free her daughter from the bondage of the demonic spirit that tormented the girl (Mark 7:24–30).

Jesus does indeed bring good news to the gentiles during His ministry, but these encounters are much more limited in scope. It is not until His resurrection that He commands His disciples to go to all nations (Matt. 28:19). As we will see in a later chapter, this corresponds to Jesus' resurrected authority as King over all.

The Church and the Kingdom

There remains one more important aspect when it comes to the people of the kingdom, and that is the relationship between the kingdom of God and the church. Are the kingdom and the church two ways of speaking of the same reality? Or is there a difference between the two?

This is a question addressed by Westminster Confession of Faith 25.2:

> The visible church, which is also catholic or universal under the gospel (not confined to one nation, as before under the law), consists of all those throughout the world that profess the true religion; and of their children: and is the kingdom of the Lord Jesus Christ, the house and family of God, out of which there is no ordinary possibility of salvation.

Notice that the confession states, "The visible church ... is the kingdom of the Lord Jesus Christ." This affirmation needs to be understood with nuance. For while we can say that the church is the kingdom, we cannot reverse that and say the kingdom is the church. What is the difference?

To understand, we need first to appreciate the differences between the kingdom and the church. The kingdom is the great end-time work of God in establishing His kingdom and rule through Christ. The church refers to the people of the kingdom: those who are renewed citizens of the kingdom.[2] The church is central to the kingdom and is like an embassy of the kingdom in this world. If you've ever visited a foreign embassy in the middle of another country, you may know that to step foot in that embassy is to set foot in the country the embassy represents. Similarly, the kingdom in this age is like the embassy of the kingdom of God, with the goal of that embassy growing larger and larger so that the kingdom of God spreads further and further in this age.

2 Cf. Ridderbos, *Coming of the Kingdom*, 354.

Despite the differences between the church and the kingdom, it is true that the church is the kingdom of Christ, and the church is the place that we should expect to find the kingdom in this age. The church is central to the kingdom. Westminster Assembly scholar Chad Van Dixhoorn states it this way: "While the kingdom of God is not the church, the church is certainly the kingdom of Jesus Christ. . . . His kingdom is bigger than the church, but it certainly includes the church."[3] This means that we should expect to find the kingdom by looking at the church, even though the kingdom is larger than the church. Yet it would not be preferable to say that the kingdom is the church because this limits the kingdom to only the people who are citizens of the kingdom. In sum, the church is the people of the kingdom, but the kingdom involves more than just the people; it refers to the rule of God in our world through Christ.

This also plays out in the mission of the church. The church's mission is more limited in scope: worshiping and making disciples.[4] The work of the kingdom, however, includes the work of the church but is also broader. The people of the kingdom are to be engaged in all sorts of righteous endeavors in this age that can be kingdom works even if they are not the mission of the church as such. In other words, the people of the kingdom should engage in spreading the

---

3 Chad Van Dixhoorn, *Confessing the Faith: A Reader's Guide to the Westminster Confession of Faith* (Banner of Truth, 2014), 341. Thanks also to Sinclair Ferguson, whose lectures on the Westminster Standards also helped clarify this issue.

4 See, e.g., Edmund P. Clowney, *The Church*, Contours of Christian Theology (IVP, 1995), 159–64; and Kevin DeYoung and Greg Gilbert, *What Is the Mission of the Church? Making Sense of Social Justice, Shalom, and the Great Commission* (Crossway, 2011), 62.

righteousness and image of God in all sorts of ways in this world, reflecting the universality of God's reign over all of life.

As the people of the kingdom, the church includes both Jews and gentiles. Citizenship in the kingdom is marked not by physical connections but by the spiritual bond of faith in Christ. This is an issue that Paul goes to great lengths to explain in his letters such as Romans, Galatians, and Ephesians. For example, Paul writes that gentile believers were formerly "alienated from the commonwealth of Israel and strangers to the covenants of promise, having no hope and without God in the world" (Eph. 2:12). But through the blood of Christ, those who were far off have come near (v. 13), with the result that they are now citizens of God's kingdom: "So then you are no longer strangers and aliens, but you are fellow citizens with the saints and members of the household of God, built on the foundation of the apostles and prophets, Christ Jesus himself being the cornerstone" (vv. 19–20).

Jews and gentiles are not natural allies, and a great division existed between them in the first century. Yet even these great barriers are overcome through faith in Christ, for He is the Savior of all peoples of the world who believe in Him, both Jews and gentiles. The church is the worldwide people of God who are citizens of the kingdom, for we serve the One who is King over the whole world.

Practical Takeaways

1. Jesus is the King of Israel, the long-awaited Son of David. This is good news for His people, who had been waiting for a king. At the same time, Jesus' kingship is good news for the world. As the true Son of David, Jesus is also the King for the whole world, not just of one small area, and His people are a worldwide people.
2. The kingdom of God does not make divisions based on worldly pedigree or background. What matters in the kingdom is not our physical heritage but faith in Christ.
3. The church is the kingdom in the sense that it is the primary place that we can expect to find the kingdom in this age. The church is the people of the kingdom who share in the blessings of the great end-time kingdom work of God through Christ.

12

The Kingdom of the Suffering Messiah

The pleasures of life are fleeting. A plate of cookies fresh from the oven doesn't stay hot for long. A cold bowl of ice cream soon melts. That vacation to a warm spot that you've been looking forward to all year lasts only a few days. Time spent with visiting family flies by in an instant. We long for the lasting joy of good things that endure.

It is easy to see how this principle also characterizes Israel's historic experience of the kingdom. So often their success was short-lived. When Joshua led the people into the promised land, they, having finally reached their goal, soon turned to idolatry. The Lord raised up judges to deliver the people, but deliverance did not last, and they were soon oppressed again.

David's victories for the Lord's kingdom did not result in permanent peace. Enemies still surrounded him, and conflict came even from within his own kingdom. Solomon established peace in a greater way, yet he faltered at the end of his life, and the kingdom split under his son. From this point, the kingdom of God struggled for stability, and the faithful looked ahead to the fulfillment of the Davidic covenant when the Lord would raise up a king who would reign forever. Jesus is that long-awaited King, but the way that He brought permanence and stability to the kingdom looked different from David's kingship.

In this chapter, we will look at the way the kingdom of God comes through Jesus, the long-awaited Messiah. The kingdom comes not through a greater military victory but through a greater, more lasting victory. Jesus is indeed a mighty warrior like His ancestor David, but He fights a bigger, more lasting battle over sin and death. And through His more powerful work, the kingdom will be permanently established.

Peter's Confession of the Christ

One of the key moments for the kingdom in the Gospels comes when Peter confesses Jesus as the Christ. In response to all that He had been doing and teaching, Jesus asked His disciples who they thought He was:

> He said to them, "But who do you say that I am?" Simon Peter replied, "You are the Christ, the Son of the living God." And Jesus answered him, "Blessed are you, Simon Bar-Jonah! For flesh and blood has not revealed this to you, but my Father who is in heaven. And I tell you, you are Peter, and on this rock I will build my church, and the gates of hell shall not prevail against it. I will give you the keys of the kingdom of heaven, and whatever you bind on earth shall be bound in heaven, and whatever you loose on earth shall be loosed in heaven." (Matt. 16:15–19)

By confessing Jesus as the Christ, Peter acknowledges that Jesus is the long-awaited Son of David who is going to rule over God's kingdom. Notice, too, that Jesus relates this confession to the triumph of the church against the gates of hell and to Apostolic authority in the kingdom of heaven. Again, we find a close relationship between the kingdom and the church.

This is a turning point in the Gospels. To this point, Jesus had been progressively revealing His messianic identity, especially to His disciples. Peter came to the correct conclusion (evident in Jesus' affirmation of his response) that Jesus is indeed the anointed King from the line of David. For Peter, this realization surely carried with it the expectation that Jesus would somehow lead a victory for the kingdom over the Roman oppressors that would recall David's victories over nations such as the Philistines. This was the precedent found in the Old Testament and the expectation that shaped the popular imagination of God's people. For example, in the noncanonical book known as the Psalms of Solomon, written sometime after the Romans captured Jerusalem in 63 BC, the coming Son of David would drive out the gentiles (that is, the Romans) from Jerusalem:

> See, Lord, and raise up for them their king, the son of David, to rule over your servant Israel in the time known to you, O God. Undergird him with the strength to destroy the unrighteous rulers, to purge Jerusalem from gentiles who trample her to destruction. (Psalms of Solomon 17:21–22)[1]

1 Translation by R.B. Wright, in *The Old Testament Pseudepigrapha*, ed. James H. Charlesworth, Anchor Bible Reference Library (Doubleday, 1983–85), 2:667.

This is not an authoritative, canonical book (nor was it written by Solomon), but it shows the sort of popular thinking during the first century that Peter was probably familiar with.

Peter's Misunderstanding About the Christ

We can surmise more of Peter's expectations in what follows when he misunderstands the nature of Jesus' messianic work. Jesus clarifies the nature of that work in the following verses of Matthew 16:

> From that time Jesus began to show his disciples that he must go to Jerusalem and suffer many things from the elders and chief priests and scribes, and be killed, and on the third day be raised. And Peter took him aside and began to rebuke him, saying, "Far be it from you, Lord! This shall never happen to you." But he turned and said to Peter, "Get behind me, Satan! You are a hindrance to me. For you are not setting your mind on the things of God, but on the things of man." (vv. 21–23)

Jesus subverts popular understandings of the messianic task by stating that He is going to suffer and be murdered in Jerusalem—quite the opposite of the victory many were hoping for! This does not fit the expected Davidic paradigm that Peter was looking for. But this is the way that the kingdom of God comes.

This is the first of the three death-and-resurrection predictions that Jesus gives, and it is significant that they come only after the disciples recognize Jesus is the Christ. This episode comes at roughly the halfway point of the Gospels. In the first half, Jesus is demonstrating that He is the Messiah through powerful deeds and words. Peter is right to recognize the messianic significance of these.

In the second half of the Gospels, Jesus is explaining the type of messiah that He is. Despite the powerful dynamic of His ministry, Jesus is not a messiah who fights a physical battle with Rome. He is instead going to give His life to ensure the permanence of God's kingdom.

This explains why, right after Peter confesses Jesus as the Christ, Jesus charges the disciples not to tell anyone (Matt. 16:20). The reason was that the disciples still did not understand the nature of Jesus' messianic work. Peter urged Jesus not to go through with this plan, but Jesus rebuked Peter to get behind Him. The kingdom was coming in a way that Peter did not expect that would involve the death of the Son of the living God.

The Purpose of Jesus' Death

In Jesus' third death-and-resurrection prediction is one of the most consequential statements Jesus gives about the purpose of His death. If we read carefully, we can relate this also to the kingdom: "For even the Son of Man came not to be served but to serve, and to give his life as a ransom for many" (Mark 10:45; see also Matt. 20:28).

To begin, we must consider who the Son of Man is. In short, this is a way for Jesus to refer to Himself. But the Old Testament background of this phrase is significant, for it comes from Daniel 7:13–14:

> "I saw in the night visions,
>
> and behold, with the clouds of heaven
> there came one like a son of man,
> and he came to the Ancient of Days
> and was presented before him.

> And to him was given dominion
> and glory and a kingdom,
> that all peoples, nations, and languages
> should serve him;
> his dominion is an everlasting dominion,
> which shall not pass away,
> and his kingdom one
> that shall not be destroyed."

This is one of the more mysterious portions of the Old Testament, but we have seen already (in chapter 3) that the book of Daniel has much to say about the fleetingness of earthly kingdoms and the permanence of the kingdom of God. The Son of Man figure in Daniel 7 adds further to that royal emphasis.

As I mentioned in chapter 3, Daniel's Son of Man rules over the permanent kingdom of God. In contrast to the other beastly kingdoms that Daniel saw in his vision, the kingdom of the Son of Man is a worldwide, everlasting dominion. This refers to the same kingdom that Nebuchadnezzar saw in his dream represented by the unhewn stone from heaven that crushes all other kingdoms (2:44–45). The Son of Man rules as a man, as One who exercises the authority originally granted to Adam in the beginning, but in a greater sense.

That Jesus preferred the term "Son of Man" for Himself is most likely a way for Him to allude to the glorious vision of the kingdom from Daniel 7. But also notice the incongruity between that vision in Daniel 7 and what Jesus says about Himself as Son of Man in Mark 10:45: He comes not to be served but to serve. The Danielic Son of Man will indeed be served by all peoples, but Jesus teaches us that first He will serve others. This He will do to the point of even laying down His own life.

Notice, too, that as Son of Man, Jesus gives His life as a ransom for many. This also derives from the Old Testament, particularly the Suffering Servant from Isaiah 53. In that context we read:

> Therefore I will divide him a portion with the many,
> and he shall divide the spoil with the strong,
> because he poured out his soul to death
> and was numbered with the transgressors;
> yet he bore the sin of many,
> and makes intercession for the transgressors. (Isa. 53:12)

This passage speaks of the Servant who gives His life to death on behalf of many, bearing their sins, and is probably the background for Mark 10:45.[2] The Suffering Servant is the Lamb who was stricken for the sins of God's people (Isa. 53:6–7).

Mark 10:45 is therefore a clear statement of the purpose of Jesus' death: It is substitutionary, given for the sins of His people. Jesus' death is not simply an example. It is not simply a motivation for us to be better people. Nor is Jesus' death an accident or something unforeseen. Instead, the death of Jesus was intentional, substitutionary, and deeply resonant with Scripture. Though it may have been surprising for Peter and the other disciples to hear that Jesus was going to suffer and die, Jesus' teaching points us back to the Old Testament.

---

2 Joel Marcus, *The Way of the Lord: Christological Exegesis of the Old Testament in the Gospel of Mark*, Studies in the New Testament and Its World (T&T Clark, 1992), 187.

This shows us that it was planned from long ago. Peter himself would later come to see this more clearly (see also 1 Peter 1:10–12).

The lasting kingdom of David, which is the glorious kingdom of the Son of Man, comes through the self-sacrifice of the Son of Man. This will lead to the everlasting dominion promised in the Old Testament. It also accords with the scriptural reality that the Son of David is also greater than David, for He is the Son of the living God.

Practical Takeaways

1. Just as the lifestyle of the kingdom is surprising in the eyes of the world, so is the pathway of the King of the kingdom. Jesus conquers not by military victory but by laying down His own life. Yet Jesus' true authority is seen in His resurrection, for death was not able to bind Him.
2. The kingdom is firmly established through the death and resurrection of Christ. Our actions do not establish the kingdom; the kingdom is established by Christ. The church prevails over the gates of Hades because of Christ, who has defeated death and hell and reigns presently from heaven.
3. To understand who Christ really is, we must be guided not by popular sentiment but by Scripture. Many people today have opinions about Jesus, but not all opinions of Jesus reflect who He truly is. Jesus is the divine Son of God who has come to earth to save us by taking to Himself a human nature without ceasing to be divine. He is one person who has two natures in the incarnation. As the divine Son of God, He saves us from the power of sin and death. As the second and last Adam, Jesus offered perfect human obedience and bore the wrath of sin throughout His life and especially on the cross. He is the God-man. (See, further, Heidelberg Catechism 16–17; Westminster Larger Catechism 38–39.)

13

The Greater David

The standards by which we assess public figures often derive from benchmarks of the past. Political leaders from bygone eras grow larger than life in the memories of their adherents. Authors from earlier generations are lionized for their genius, and their works become unassailable. Records set by generational athletes of previous years are the test of athletes today. And so it goes.

When it comes to the kingdom, David was the paradigm of the great king in Israel's memory. He was the mighty, godly leader who led the people in righteousness and brought great success for God's people. David established the kingdom and captured Jerusalem. David prepared for the building of God's temple. David authored many of the psalms. And it was with David that the Lord made a covenant promising an everlasting dynasty.

But as great as David was, his coming Son would be greater than he was. The coming King would be not only David's son but also David's Lord (Ps. 110:1). This is a mysterious truth that comes into fuller focus in the Gospels.

The Triumphal Entry

The Promised Son of David

The second half of the Gospels features Jesus teaching His disciples what sort of messiah He is, and this comes into full view when He comes to Jerusalem as a King in the triumphal entry. Jesus sent His disciples to find a colt on which no one had ever sat and bring it to Him so that He could enter Jerusalem.

To enter Jerusalem in this way, seated on a new colt, was not simply the normal way to get around in the ancient world. This was not the ancient equivalent of hailing a taxicab or a ride share. Like so much of Jesus' ministry, this was a highly symbolic moment demonstrating the nature of the kingdom.

By entering Jerusalem on a colt, Jesus was announcing with clarity that He was the long-awaited Son of David who would usher in God's kingdom. This is apparent in the people's response to this action:

> And many spread their cloaks on the road, and others spread leafy branches that they had cut from the fields. And those who went before and those who followed were shouting, "Hosanna! Blessed is he who comes in the name of the Lord! Blessed is the coming kingdom of our father David! Hosanna in the highest!" (Mark 11:8–10)

Luke's gospel includes other aspects of what the people said: "Blessed is the King who comes in the name of the Lord! Peace in heaven and glory in the highest!" (Luke 19:38).

The people recognize Jesus' actions as a royal demonstration, and their jubilant response of "Hosanna" echoes Psalm 118:

> Open to me the gates of righteousness,
> that I may enter through them
> and give thanks to the LORD.
> This is the gate of the LORD;
> the righteous shall enter through it.
> I thank you that you have answered me
> and have become my salvation.
> The stone that the builders rejected
> has become the cornerstone.
> This is the LORD's doing;
> it is marvelous in our eyes.
> This is the day that the LORD has made;
> let us rejoice and be glad in it.
>
> Save us, we pray, O LORD!
> O LORD, we pray, give us success! (vv. 19–25)

In this psalm we hear the voice of the King who leads His people out of bondage, celebrating the Lord's salvation.[1] This psalm looks back to the earlier deliverance of God's people and anticipates a future day of deliverance as well. The crowd's cry "Hosanna" comes from the Hebrew phrasing "Save us" (see Ps. 118:25).

Psalm 118 celebrates the past but also prophetically looks forward to the day that the King—the rejected stone—would become

1 See Waltke and Zaspel, *How to Read*, 395–96.

the cornerstone. The New Testament makes it clear that Jesus is the rejected cornerstone, but He is proved to be precious in His resurrection (see Acts 4:11; 1 Peter 2:7).[2] The day of rejoicing this psalm looks ahead to is the day of the glorification of the Messiah, when the kingdom would be reestablished.

The triumphal entry is therefore of the King who is coming to reestablish God's kingdom in a new way. Jesus embraces and encourages this activity: riding into Jerusalem as a King and affirming the children when they later cried out, "Hosanna to the Son of David!" (see Matt. 21:14–16). In what follows in this last week of Jesus' life, He will speak more forthrightly about who He really is and will eventually give His life to establish this kingdom; He will suffer, be crucified, and then subsequently be raised from the dead. The stone rejected by the builders would become the cornerstone.

Political Kingdom?

Jesus' royal entrance into Jerusalem leads to one of the perennial questions about the kingdom of God: Is it political? A nuanced answer is required. Is the kingdom political? Yes and no, depending on what the questioner means.

Yes, the kingdom is political in the sense that Jesus is the King of all kings, and He rules over a kingdom that will last forever. He is the King of Israel, but His dominion extends beyond Israel to encompass people from around the world. When we serve Jesus, we are paying homage to the King of Israel, recognizing that this kingdom will last forever. His people are citizens of His kingdom, and they owe fealty to him as King. He also gives us, as we have seen in the Sermon on

2 See again Waltke and Zaspel, *How to Read*, 395.

the Mount and elsewhere, a code of conduct for what it looks like to live in this kingdom.

At the same time, the kingdom is not political if by that we mean that the kingdom of God is correlated to any earthly country, government, or political party of this age. It is not. The kingdom of God does not simply plug into current earthly administrations—it transcends them. The kingdom is the stone that comes from heaven and crushes all other kingdoms. No earthly government or nation will last forever; all will eventually be crushed by the everlasting kingdom of God.

Even so, Jesus teaches us that it is possible to be both a faithful member of an earthly kingdom and a faithful member of the kingdom of God. This is one implication of His memorable phrase about the coin: "Render to Caesar the things that are Caesar's, and to God the things that are God's" (Mark 12:17). It was not always assumed in Jesus' day that a person could do both (nor perhaps today), but Jesus shows us that it is possible. Yet the caveat is that sometimes earthly governments set themselves up against the Lord and against His Anointed (see Ps. 2:2); in such circumstances, a person may not be able to serve faithfully both God and the earthly government. A Christian must choose between faithfulness to the Lord and faithfulness to man (see Acts 4:19; 5:29). The book of Revelation is one biblical text that guides God's people in such circumstances.

It is also important to note the benefits of Jesus' kingship. The Westminster Shorter Catechism summarizes:

> 26. How does Christ execute the office of a king?
>
> Christ executes the office of a king, in subduing us to Himself, in ruling and defending us, and in restraining and conquering all His and our enemies.

As our King, Jesus guides us in righteousness and leads us to an everlasting inheritance. He is powerful enough to defeat the kingdom of Satan, forgive our sins, and grant us everlasting life. As the true King of kings, Jesus grants us blessings that are more permanent than the passing privileges of this age.

We see the interplay between Jesus' kingship and the spiritual blessings that He bestows in the song of Zechariah, the father of John the Baptist:

> "Blessed be the Lord God of Israel,
> for he has visited and redeemed his people
> and has raised up a horn of salvation for us
> in the house of his servant David,
> as he spoke by the mouth of his holy prophets from of old,
> that we should be saved from our enemies
> and from the hand of all who hate us;
> to show the mercy promised to our fathers
> and to remember his holy covenant,
> the oath that he swore to our father Abraham, to grant us
> that we, being delivered from the hand of our enemies,
> might serve him without fear,
> in holiness and righteousness before him all our days."
> (Luke 1:68–75)

The "horn of salvation" in verse 69 refers to the strength of the coming King from David's line, which Jesus fulfills. This King will save God's people from their enemies (vv. 71, 74) and show mercy to God's people (v. 72), that they may serve Him without fear (v. 74). Yet, as we have seen, Jesus does not grant these things by fighting an earthly, military battle. Instead, Jesus fights a more profound battle, defeating the spiritual forces of evil (see 1 John 3:8). (Zechariah's statements are in the past tense because they are absolutely certain, even though from Zechariah's perspective they had yet to be accomplished.) Zechariah then continues, noting that God's salvation includes the forgiveness of sins (v. 77). This is indeed a different type of kingship that transcends what any earthly king can grant.

David's Son and David's Lord

This different kingdom that Jesus brings points again to His status as the greater Son of David. The triumphal entry marks the final week of Jesus' earthly life, and from this point on He speaks with much more clarity about who He is. For example, whereas earlier in the Gospels the phrase "Son of Man" is veiled in mystery, by the last time this phrase appears in Matthew and Mark, Jesus relates it to the Son of Man passage in Daniel 7:13–14. In response to the high priest's accusatory question "Are you the Christ, the Son of the Blessed?" Jesus responds, "I am, and you will see the Son of Man seated at the right hand of Power, and coming with the clouds of heaven" (Mark 14:61–62). The phrase "coming with the clouds" is from Daniel 7:13 and refers to the glory of the Son of Man who rules over an everlasting kingdom (v. 14). Here Jesus clarifies the mystery of how we should understand "Son of Man" and points to His role as the ruler over the kingdom of God.

The other Old Testament text that Jesus invokes in Mark 14:62 is Psalm 110:1: The Son of Man will be seated at the right hand of God. This points to the coming glorification of Jesus when He will be raised from the dead and ascend into heaven, ruling at God's right hand until He returns.

Psalm 110:1 is the same text that Jesus uses earlier during Passion Week to speak of His status that is greater than David's:

> And as Jesus taught in the temple, he said, "How can the scribes say that the Christ is the son of David? David himself, in the Holy Spirit, declared,
>
> "'The Lord said to my Lord,
> "Sit at my right hand,
> until I put your enemies under your feet."'
>
> David himself calls him Lord. So how is he his son?" And the great throng heard him gladly. (Mark 12:35–37)

Psalm 110 is indeed wonderfully mysterious. Who is the Lord who spoke to the Lord? In the Greek of the Gospels, the word for "Lord" is the same word in both instances. But in the Hebrew original of Psalm 110:1, two different words for "Lord" are used, making it clear that two distinct persons are in view: one "Lord" who speaks to another "Lord."

This psalm prophetically looks to one who is both David's Son—that is, the offspring from the line of David who would eventually rule over his kingdom forever—and David's Lord. From the New Testament witness, we learn that David's Lord must be the divine Son of God who existed before David and who is inherently greater than David. Jesus is this Son of God who is David's Lord. His sitting at God's right hand looks ahead to His glorification, when He will reign at God's right hand as the authoritative Messiah until He comes again as the Judge of all.

Jesus' opponents had no answer to His challenge about this psalm (see Matt. 22:46), because the correct interpretation of it must recognize that Jesus uniquely fulfills this. Only Jesus is both David's Son and David's Lord. He was born of Mary into the royal line of David, but this was not His beginning. To build on the practical takeaways from the previous chapter: Jesus has existed eternally as the eternal Son of God. It was only "in the fullness of time" that He took a human nature in the incarnation, but He has always been the eternal Son of God. In the incarnation, He became what He formerly was not (a man) without ceasing to be what He always has been (the eternal Son of God). Jesus is God come to save us, for only God can save us from the perils of sin (see John 10:17–18; Titus 2:13–14). But He also came as man to save us, for only a man can undo the curse of Adam and fulfill the conditions for eternal life (see Rom. 5:12–21; 1 Cor. 15:21).

The mystery of the incarnation is great. Who can understand these things fully? Yet what a glorious truth that the eternal Son of God became the Son of David so that He may save His people from their sins. He is greater than David; He is greater than any person who has ever lived. Only Jesus is the divine Son of God who is also truly man. He is a Messiah worth serving!

Practical Takeaways

1. Our highest priority in this age is to live faithfully as citizens of the kingdom of God. The kingdom of God transcends all other kingdoms. How we live as citizens of the kingdom of God should nevertheless affect the way that we live in earthly kingdoms. We are to live peaceable and quiet lives and pray for the good of the

kingdoms in which we live (1 Tim. 2:1–2; 1 Peter 2:13–17). It is quite possible to be faithful earthly citizens and faithful citizens of the kingdom of God. But we also need to keep clear our highest priority and recognize that no earthly kingdom lasts forever. If we are confronted with a fundamental conflict between heavenly and earthly citizenship, we must obey God rather than man.

2. Our hope should therefore not be in any political entity or party; no earthly leader can bring the lasting change that our world truly needs. Our world—and each of us—needs the new life that comes only through Christ. Even so, we are not called to isolate ourselves from the world. Kingdom citizens, as those spread throughout the earth in their various callings, should be actively engaged in all manner of noble works in this age, consistent with the calling to be kingdom citizens.
3. The relationship between the kingdom of God and earthly kingdoms is notoriously debated, and I cannot answer all these questions here. One point to make: When we pray "Thy kingdom come" in the Lord's Prayer, we are praying that God's will would be done on earth, which has implications for all of life, including the earthly political realm. But we also must remember that the kingdom of God is not to be identified with any earthly government or society; it transcends them, even as it has implications for how we live with respect to them.

14

The Death of the King

History is full of examples of kingdoms that fell or faltered after their leaders died. One example is Alexander the Great. As we saw in chapter 3, Alexander conquered much of the world from Greece to North Africa to India. Yet his kingdom was spread thin and did not last long. When Alexander died at age thirty-two, his massive kingdom soon split into four subkingdoms that warred among themselves. His kingdom did not thrive after his death.

The same is not true for Jesus. His kingdom prospers after His death. Although Peter tried to hinder Jesus from going to Jerusalem to die, it was through Jesus' death that the kingdom would be fully established. By His death, Jesus sealed His perfect work and gave His life as a substitutionary sacrifice to defeat sin and death.

Jesus' death was not the end of His kingdom. Though Jesus truly died and remained under the power of death for a time, death did not have the last word on Jesus. The reason that His death saves us and establishes the kingdom is that Jesus overcame death through

His resurrection. In this chapter, we will relate the death of Christ to the kingdom. There is obviously much we can say about the death of Christ, but our primary focus will be on how it secures His kingdom. Christ's death cannot be viewed as an isolated event; we must understand it in consideration of His victorious resurrection. Both are important for understanding the securing of His kingdom. This present chapter must be read in tandem with chapter 15, where I will say more about the resurrection and the kingdom of God.

The Last Supper and the Kingdom

The Last Supper of Jesus with His disciples occurs the night before Jesus' crucifixion. Earlier, we saw from the Gospel of Mark that in the miracle of the feeding of the five thousand and later in the feeding of the four thousand, the bread represented Jesus' body (6:31–44; 8:1–9). Later, Mark tells us the disciples were fearful during a storm because they did not yet understand about the bread (6:52), and Jesus reminded the disciples of the number of baskets left over each time that He fed the multitudes (8:14–21). To understand rightly about the bread is to understand rightly about Jesus. We have also seen that Jesus' death was intentional, and He viewed His death as a substitutionary offering in fulfillment of Isaiah 53 (see Matt. 20:28; Mark 10:45).

Therefore, when we come to the Last Supper in the Gospels, Jesus has already made it clear that the bread is significant for the way that it points to His person and work, and His death is intended to save His people from their sins. Jesus builds on these themes in His explanation of the meaning of the Last Supper and relates it to the coming kingdom of God:

> Now as they were eating, Jesus took bread, and after blessing it broke it and gave it to the disciples, and said, "Take, eat; this is my body." And he took a cup, and when he had given thanks he gave it to them, saying, "Drink of it, all of you, for this is my blood of the covenant, which is poured out for many for the forgiveness of sins. I tell you I will not drink again of this fruit of the vine until that day when I drink it new with you in my Father's kingdom." (Matt. 26:26–29)

Here again, the body of Jesus is represented by bread, and Jesus institutes the Lord's Supper as a way to remember His work and presence with us in perpetuity. The bread represents the body of Jesus. The wine represents His blood. Just as the bread was broken at the meal and ingested, and just as they drank the wine—and just as we continue to do these things today in memory of this event—so can we be sure that Jesus has given Himself for us that our sins would be forgiven (see Heidelberg Catechism 79).

Notice, too, the relationship that Jesus makes between these words of institution of the Last Supper and the kingdom: Jesus will not drink of the fruit of the vine again until He drinks it with His disciples in His Father's kingdom (Matt. 26:29). This points to a future date when Jesus will return as the King and consummate the kingdom. We partake of the Lord's Supper in perpetuity until Christ returns, as Paul teaches us (1 Cor. 11:26). When Christ returns as King, He will again eat with His disciples in a wonderful banquet of consummation.

This promise already assumes something important about the death of Christ: Death is not the last word. Jesus will rise victorious over the grave on the third day. It will be as the risen and ascended One that Christ will return to sup with His disciples in the newness of the kingdom.

Here Jesus speaks about forgiveness of sins and a new covenant in language that recalls the new covenant spoken of by the prophet Jeremiah (Jer. 31:31–34). This covenant is often rightly associated with the forgiveness of sins, for Jeremiah explicitly mentions this benefit (v. 34). But it is also helpful to remember that the blessings of the new era are not one-dimensional; they also include the restoration of the kingship and the kingdom (see also v. 38). Jeremiah's prophecy of a new covenant comes in a context in which Jerusalem is going to fall because of the sinfulness of the people who had violated the Lord's covenant (5:14–19). He thus predicts a new covenant that will not be broken (31:32–33). The result of their broken covenant (the Mosaic covenant) was a broken kingdom; no son of David was ruling victoriously on the throne. When the new covenant comes, the people will be forgiven for their sins, and the Son of David will rule victoriously on the throne (see 23:1–6).

The need for forgiveness of sins correlates also to the need for a reestablished kingdom. Jesus points to His actions in the Last Supper—which look forward to His impending death—as the means for finally and fully addressing the sin of the broken covenant. His death was not the final defeat but was the means of inaugurating the new covenant promised by Jeremiah. His death brings forgiveness of sins and the new covenant and is how the kingdom is permanently established.

The Arrest of the King

After the Last Supper, Jesus goes with His disciples to pray in the garden of Gethsemane. It is at this juncture that Judas the betrayer arrives with a cadre of soldiers from the chief priest to arrest Jesus (John 18:1–3). Even in this moment of great darkness, however, the King is in control, and His kingdom is coming.

In the Gospel of John, the soldiers (perhaps hundreds)[1] fall prostrate to the ground when Jesus approaches and says, "I am He"—which could also be translated simply "I am." This is the final of seven "I am" statements in John (a rich number indeed) that illustrate Jesus' divine authority. The soldiers could not arrest Jesus unless He allowed them to, which correlates to what Jesus already said earlier in the Gospel of John: No one takes Jesus' life from Him; He has the authority to lay down His life, and He has the authority to take it up again (John 10:17–18).

Jesus is indeed arrested in the garden, but only Jesus is arrested—the disciples are allowed to go free. This fulfills Scripture, as we read in the Gospel of Matthew: "Then Jesus said to them, 'You will all fall away because of me this night. For it is written, "I will strike the shepherd, and the sheep of the flock will be scattered"'" (Matt. 26:31). This is a quotation from Zechariah 13:7, which anticipates a day when the coming Son of David would be struck. The shepherd in Zechariah 13 refers to the royal leader of God's people, which (as we have already seen in the Gospels) is an image that Jesus uses for His role in bringing the kingdom (see 1 Kings 22:17; Ezek. 34:5 in Matt. 9:35–36). Jesus is the messianic Shepherd who lays down His life so that not one of the sheep would be lost (John 18:9). But His death will not be the last word, for He also tells His disciples, "But after I am raised up, I will go before

1 See Craig S. Keener, *The Gospel of John: A Commentary* (Hendrickson, 2003), 2:1080.

you to Galilee" (Matt. 26:32). The crucified Christ would rise and meet His disciples in Galilee.

A Kingdom Not of This World

After His arrest, Jesus is taken first to the high priest and then to Pilate, where He is put on trial. Before Caiaphas (the high priest) and the Sanhedrin (the Jewish council), Jesus is questioned about His kingship. They ask Him if He is the Christ—that is, whether He is the royal Son of David (Matt. 26:63; Mark 14:61; Luke 22:66). Yet they do not ask sincerely but ask only to condemn Him (see Luke 22:67).

There is more to the high priest's questioning: He asks not only if Jesus is the Christ but also if He is the Son of God (Matt. 26:63; Mark 14:61). It is at this juncture that Jesus responds with a combination of Daniel 7:13 and Psalm 110:1, as we saw in the previous chapter: "And Jesus said, 'I am, and you will see the Son of Man seated at the right hand of Power, and coming with the clouds of heaven'" (Mark 14:62). Here the high priest apparently inquired of Jesus if He claimed to be more than just a natural son of David, for his response is that Jesus had just committed blasphemy (Matt. 26:63–65; Mark 14:63–64). Yet it was not blasphemy. It is true; Jesus is the Christ, the Son of God.

Since the Jewish leaders did not have the authority under Roman occupation to put anyone to death legally, they then shipped Jesus off to Pontius Pilate, the Roman governor. To Pilate, Jesus explained in more detail the nature of His person and kingship. Pilate's line of questioning centered on whether Jesus was the King of the Jews (Matt. 27:11; Mark 15:2; Luke 23:3). If Jesus was setting Himself up as king, this would have been viewed as rebellion against Rome, for no one was allowed to challenge the kingship of Caesar (see Luke 23:2). But even in this context we see that Jesus is truly Lord of all (see Acts 10:36), as Jesus explains to Pilate the nature of His kingdom:

> So Pilate entered his headquarters again and called Jesus and said to him, "Are you the King of the Jews?" Jesus answered, "Do you say this of your own accord, or did others say it to you about me?" Pilate answered, "Am I a Jew? Your own nation and the chief priests have delivered you over to me. What have you done?" Jesus answered, "My kingdom is not of this world. If my kingdom were of this world, my servants would have been fighting, that I might not be delivered over to the Jews. But my kingdom is not from the world." Then Pilate said to him, "So you are a king?" Jesus answered, "You say that I am a king. For this purpose I was born and for this purpose I have come into the world—to bear witness to the truth. Everyone who is of the truth listens to my voice." (John 18:33–37)

This is one of only two passages in John that use the language of "kingdom" for the work of Jesus. Though Jesus is on trial, he speaks boldly and authoritatively before Pilate. Jesus, in effect, challenges Pilate's line of questioning and speaks about His prior existence and coming into the world.

Notice that Jesus does not deny being a king, but He denies that His kingdom is "of this world." This is not to say that the kingdom of God does not make an impact in the world, but the kingdom of God does not come in a worldly way and is not characterized by the structures, values, and characteristics of worldly kingdoms. Jesus' kingdom does not come by physical force, which is why Jesus' disciples were not taking up arms on His behalf—something Peter got wrong in the garden of Gethsemane (see John 18:10–11).

Instead, Jesus' kingdom is a heavenly kingdom. His kingdom comes not by guarding His life at all costs but by laying down His life so that His kingdom would be established. Though the Sanhedrin and Pilate may have thought that they were hindering the kingdom from coming, they were actually the means for God's predetermined plan to come to pass (see Acts 2:23). By laying down His life and taking it up again, Jesus firmly establishes His heavenly kingdom on earth.

Jesus' authority was beyond anything that Pilate had ever encountered as a Roman governor. When told later by the Jews that Jesus claimed to be the Son of God, Pilate asked Jesus where He was from, but Jesus did not answer (John 19:7–9). When Pilate asked Jesus, "Do you not know that I have authority to release you and authority to crucify you?" (v. 10), Jesus answered, "You would have no authority over me at all unless it had been given you from above" (v. 11). From that point, Pilate sought to release Jesus, but he eventually resigned himself to the will of the crowd.

The irony about kingship in this encounter is thick; the people's actions reflect a tragic misunderstanding of the reality before them. The people tell Pilate—the representative of the Roman emperor—that if he does not have Jesus crucified, then Pilate is no friend of Caesar. In this scenario, the Jewish agitators side with the Roman occupiers and the Roman definition of kingship (which is a far cry from the precedent of King David) rather than siding with their true King. They reject Jesus, their rightful King, and turn instead to the Romans, even proclaiming, "We have no king but Caesar" (John 19:15). Yet the irony is that Jesus is indeed the true King, and by rejecting Him they set the course of events that will lead to the permanent establishment of His kingdom through His death and resurrection. Here the Jewish representatives have rejected King Jesus and chosen to side with Caesar instead of God's true Anointed One. Anything to get rid of the perceived threat of Jesus.

They succeed in having Jesus crucified, but they fail in impeding His kingdom. By His death, the kingdom is established.

The Crucifixion of the King

After Jesus is condemned to death, His kingship is mocked. Again, the scene is ironic; those who mock Him treat Him as a faux king when, in fact, He is the King of all kings. They give Him a scepter, dress Him in a purple robe, place on His head a painful crown of thorns, and prostrate themselves in derisive homage (Matt. 27:27–31; Mark 15:16–20; John 19:1–5). Pilate mocks Jesus' kingship before the crowd, proclaiming, "Behold the man!" (John 19:5), in language that mocked Jesus' kingship. This perhaps is even portrayed by John as a recollection of the first royal man in the beginning, Adam (see Gen. 3:22).[2] If this is the case, John may be helping us see that Jesus is the last Adam, who through His death undoes the sin of the first Adam.

The Gospels continue to present Jesus' kingship on the cross. The cross was a shameful tool of torture and execution used by the Romans that was particularly designed for political revolutionaries. The words identifying the two men crucified on either side of Jesus

2 M. David Litwa, "Behold Adam: A Reading of John 19:5," *Horizons in Biblical Theology* 32 (2010): 142, followed by Edward W. Klink III, *John*, Zondervan Exegetical Commentary on the New Testament 4 (Zondervan, 2016), 778–79.

are often translated as "robbers" or "thieves" (Matt. 27:38; Mark 15:27). Yet the Greek term (*lēstai*) in context may perhaps be better translated as "political rebels."[3] Barabbas, the prisoner who was released instead of Jesus, was also a political revolutionary (Mark 15:7; John 18:40). That Jesus was crucified between two *lēstai* further highlights the kingdom-related charge against Jesus: He was crucified on trumped-up charges of leading a rival kingdom to Caesar's. Though the trial was a sham and Jesus' kingdom is not of this world, it is indeed true that He brings a kingdom that overcomes all other kingdoms, and this He brings by His death.

It is therefore fitting that the title posted above Jesus on the cross read, "Jesus of Nazareth, the King of the Jews" (John 19:19). Again, the ironic reality is that Jesus really is the King of the Jews, though He was crucified unjustly as One who was perceived *not* to be the true King. Further, this title was written in Latin, Aramaic, and Greek, the three most common languages of the era in this region. The title thus intimates that Jesus is not only the King of the Jews but also the King for the whole world.

Before Jesus breathes out His last, He takes the words of Psalm 22:1 on His lips, which He uniquely fulfills: "My God, my God, why have you forsaken me?" (Matt. 27:46; Mark 15:34). Here Jesus suffers, as the representative man and Son of David, bearing the wrath of God against human sin. This is a moment of intense agony. Yet that agony would not be the last word. Psalm 22 moves from lament

3 See Walter Bauer, *A Greek-English Lexicon of the New Testament and Other Early Christian Literature* (BDAG), 3rd ed., ed. Frederick W. Danker (Chicago: University of Chicago, 2000), 594; and N.T. Wright, *Jesus and the Victory of God*, Christian Origins and the Question of God 2 (Fortress, 1996), 155, 419–20, 546.

to praise, with David eventually proclaiming he will praise the Lord in the congregation (Ps. 22:22; see also Heb. 2:12) and recognizing that the Lord is truly King over all the nations (Ps. 22:27–28).

The death of Jesus is therefore not His final defeat; it is the appointed path for ushering in the kingdom that will outlast all other kingdoms. It is therefore appropriate that when Jesus breathed out His last, the Roman centurion at the cross recognized, "Truly this man was the Son of God!" (Mark 15:39).

Practical Takeaways

1. Followers of Christ should not expect congratulations from the world. We hold to a countercultural message of sin and our need for deliverance, and we follow a King whose kingdom does not play by the rules of this world. Jesus was faithful unto death even though He never sinned; He was treated unjustly. Followers of Jesus should therefore not expect to be treated better than our holy King. Let us therefore remain faithful, even in the face of injustice (see 1 Peter 2:19–23).
2. Jesus' death and resurrection not only establish the kingdom but are also the way sins are atoned for. Jesus has paid the penalty for the sins of all who look to Him in faith, and His vindication from death is the guarantee that all those who are in Christ will also be delivered from death. Kingdom citizens are forgiven sinners.
3. The Lord's Supper is the covenant meal that Jesus has given to us to commemorate His death and look forward to His return. It is a perpetual meal that reminds us of what Jesus has done and that He will be with us

to the end of the age. To participate in the supper well means that we must examine ourselves, receive the Word preached, and feed on Christ by faith.

15

The Resurrection and the Spread of the Kingdom

One of the most famous radio voices of the twentieth century belonged to Paul Harvey, who for many years brought listeners *The Rest of the Story*. These radio vignettes provided inspirational insights into people and events that we might not otherwise know—often heartwarming, often surprising.

In this chapter, we will consider "the rest of the story" after the cross of Christ. Christian tradition often features the cross as a focal point—and rightly so. Jesus has much to say about the importance of His suffering and death, and Paul magnifies the glories of the cross through which we are saved from our sins. The cross is in many ways the summary focal point of the love of Christ for us and represents the culmination of His sacrificial work.

Yet we also do well to remember that the cross is not the end of the story of Christ. If Jesus had died on the cross and the Gospels had ended with His death, then the enemies of Jesus would have triumphed over Him. Paul tells us that if Christ has not risen from the dead, then we are still in our sins (1 Cor. 15:17). But thankfully, we have the rest of the story about how Jesus overcame death through His glorious resurrection.

By His resurrection, Jesus has defeated sin and conquered its last sting by overcoming death (1 Cor. 15:54–57). As the presently exalted Lord, Jesus fulfills the Davidic covenant by reigning over the promised everlasting kingdom, and since He rules from heaven, He rules over the world. Jesus lives today and will one day return to earth to rule over His consummated kingdom.

The Kingdom Comes with Power

One of the more mysterious statements Jesus makes about the kingdom comes in Mark 8:38–9:1. In the context of His three death-and-resurrection predictions—along with His instructions on the nature of discipleship in the kingdom of God—Jesus says:

> "For whoever is ashamed of me and of my words in this adulterous and sinful generation, of him will the Son of Man also be ashamed when he comes in the glory of his Father with the holy angels."
>
> And he said to them, "Truly, I say to you, there are some standing here who will not taste death until they see the kingdom of God after it has come with power."

Jesus relates His coming as Son of Man in glory and with angels to the coming of the kingdom of God in power. Jesus' coming with the angels refers to His future return in glory, and so it sounds as though Jesus is saying that some of His disciples who were standing there with Him would not die before Jesus comes a second time in glory. Jesus was not wrong about this. It is true. We know now that Jesus has not yet returned in glory. So what was Jesus referring to?

The answer must come from the immediate context. Right after Jesus says some of His disciples would soon see the kingdom of God come in power, something remarkable happens:

> After six days Jesus took with him Peter and James and John, and led them up a high mountain by themselves. And he was transfigured before them, and his clothes became radiant, intensely white, as no one on earth could bleach them. And there appeared to them Elijah with Moses, and they were talking with Jesus. And Peter said to Jesus, "Rabbi, it is good that we are here. Let us make three tents, one for you and one for Moses and one for Elijah." For he did not know what to say, for they were terrified. And a cloud overshadowed them, and a voice came out of the cloud, "This is my beloved Son; listen to him." And suddenly, looking around, they no longer saw anyone with them but Jesus only. (Mark 9:2–8)

This event, known as the transfiguration, is important for understanding the kingdom of God. The glorious radiance of Jesus that is on display in this event is reflective of His true glory as the eternal Son of God. Jesus' glory is His own, whereas the glory that Moses reflected during his earthly life was reflective of God's glory. Further, both Moses and Elijah had the privilege to experience a theophany, or appearance of God. Yet in this account, the second person of the Trinity stands before them in glory.

But there is another angle to the transfiguration as well: This event also points ahead to the kingdom's future coming in glory.

This is how Jesus frames the event in Mark 9:1: Jesus' disciples saw the glory of Jesus, which was a preview and guarantee of the glory that Jesus will manifest when He returns to consummate the kingdom. This is how Peter later explains the significance of the transfiguration:

> For we did not follow cleverly devised myths when we made known to you the power and coming of our Lord Jesus Christ, but we were eyewitnesses of his majesty. For when he received honor and glory from God the Father, and the voice was borne to him by the Majestic Glory, "This is my beloved Son, with whom I am well pleased," we ourselves heard this very voice borne from heaven, for we were with him on the holy mountain. (2 Peter 1:16–18)

Peter was present on the Mount of Transfiguration, and he explains in his second letter that the glory of Jesus manifested in the transfiguration is the same glory that will be manifested when Jesus comes again. The transfiguration is, therefore, a preview of the future glory of the King that will be revealed when He comes to consummate the kingdom. Peter therefore points to the transfiguration as proof that Jesus really is going to return; His return is not a fable or a myth. But just as surely as the glory of Jesus was revealed on the Mount of Transfiguration, so surely will Jesus return in glory.

This is what it means to see the kingdom of God come with power. The disciples saw a preview of the future power and glory of the kingdom because they saw a preview of the glory Jesus manifests in His state of exaltation beginning with His resurrection. The transfiguration is therefore also a preview of the resurrection glory of Jesus.

The Resurrection of the King

The resurrection is crucial to the logic of the gospel narratives. Jesus three times predicts His own death and resurrection, His resurrection is previewed in the transfiguration, and He states that He has the authority both to lay down His life and to take it up again (John 10:17–18). He also tells His disciples that after He is raised, He will meet them in Galilee (Matt. 26:32; Mark 14:28; 16:7). Jesus' words are sure, and His predictions of His resurrection are not vain. They are fulfilled. He did rise from the dead, and He did go before His disciples to Galilee.

The resurrection, therefore, resolves the gospel narratives and provides much of the logic for how Jesus reigns over an everlasting kingdom. Earlier we saw that after Peter confessed Jesus as the long-awaited King, he urged Jesus not to go to Jerusalem to die and rise again (Matt. 16:21–23). Peter did not understand the nature of Jesus' kingship, but by dying and rising again, Jesus defeats the devil, sin, and death and rules forever, never to die again.

When Jesus rises from the dead, His message is updated to reflect His authority as the risen One. It is in this context that we come to a passage that may be familiar:

> Now the eleven disciples went to Galilee, to the mountain to which Jesus had directed them. And when they saw him they worshiped him, but some doubted. And Jesus came and said to them, "All authority in heaven and on earth has been given to me. Go therefore and make disciples of all nations, baptizing them in the name of the Father and of the Son and of the Holy Spirit, teaching them to observe all that I have commanded you. And behold, I am with you always, to the end of the age." (Matt. 28:16–20)

In this Great Commission, Jesus claims all authority in heaven and on earth. This reflects His authority as the risen One. It is not that Jesus did not have authority before this as the eternal Son of God. But Jesus is referring especially to the accomplishment of His work of suffering and His victory by means of His resurrection. Jesus speaks here as the King who has conquered. Jesus has often spoken of Himself in the Gospels as the Son of Man—often as the suffering Son of Man—but here He speaks of Himself as the victorious, conquering Son of Man. He speaks of His authority in a way that recalls the kingdom of the Son of Man from Daniel 7:14:

> "And to him [i.e., the Son of Man] was given dominion
> and glory and a kingdom,
> that all peoples, nations, and languages
> should serve him;
> his dominion is an everlasting dominion,
> which shall not pass away,
> and his kingdom one
> that shall not be destroyed."

Jesus is the fulfillment of the vision that Daniel saw of a King who will reign over all other kingdoms. Though Jesus' ministry seemed to His disciples to have ended in the disappointment of His execution, His subsequent resurrection demonstrates the surpassing greatness of His person and kingdom. No earthly king can hold a candle to Him, for He is King of kings and Lord of lords (Rev. 17:14).

Something else happens when Jesus is raised from the dead. Whereas Jesus' earthly ministry was focused mostly on Israel, in His resurrected state Jesus expressly tells His disciples to go to *all* nations.

As the resurrected King of Israel, Jesus is also the new Adam. He not only restores the kingdom to Israel and rules in place of His ancestor David, but He also brings life in place of death to anyone from any nation who would come to Him. The resurrection is crucial to the kingdom of God.

The Heavenly Exaltation of the King

The Gospels tell us that Jesus is the resurrected King with authority over all. But the logic of the kingdom also includes the heavenly exaltation of the King. After Jesus' resurrection appearances to His disciples, Jesus ascended into heaven (see Luke 24:50–51). Jesus' ascension is also key for understanding the kingdom of God, for Jesus ascended to the right hand of God, where He presently reigns in anticipation of His future return.

This aspect of the reign of Christ finds greater explanation in the book of Acts. On the day of Pentecost, when the Holy Spirit was mightily poured out on God's people, Peter explained that the powerful working of the Spirit was proof that Jesus has been exalted as the Son of David:

> "Brothers, I may say to you with confidence about the patriarch David that he both died and was buried, and his tomb is with us to this day. Being therefore a prophet, and knowing that God had sworn with an oath to him that he would set one of his descendants on his throne, he foresaw and spoke about the resurrection of the Christ, that he was not abandoned to Hades, nor did his flesh see corruption. This Jesus God raised up, and of that we all are witnesses. Being therefore exalted at the right hand of God, and having received from the Father the promise of the Holy Spirit, he

> has poured out this that you yourselves are seeing and hearing. For David did not ascend into the heavens, but he himself says,
>
> > "'The Lord said to my Lord,
> > "Sit at my right hand,
> > until I make your enemies your footstool."'
> > [quoting Ps. 110:1]
>
> Let all the house of Israel therefore know for certain that God has made him both Lord and Christ, this Jesus whom you crucified." (Acts 2:29–36)

The focus on David in this passage highlights the kingship of Christ. David did not reign forever, but he was promised a descendant who would reign forever. David remained in the grave, so when he wrote in Psalm 16 that he would not be abandoned to the grave (see Acts 2:25–28), he was speaking prophetically about his greater Son who would not be left in the grave. He was speaking about the resurrection of Christ.

Further, Peter explained that the resurrected Christ had also ascended into heaven, fulfilling Psalm 110:1. Peter concludes that Jesus has been made both Lord and Christ. This "made" does not mean that Jesus was neither Lord nor Christ before His resurrection (cf. Luke 2:11). But the "made" means that Jesus has been installed as the heavenly Lord and messianic King. This means that Jesus reigns now from heaven. The kingdom of God is presently ruled by a heavenly King.

Similarly, later in Acts, the Apostle Paul relates the present heavenly reign of Jesus to the fulfillment of Scripture:

> "And we bring you the good news that what God promised to the fathers, this he has fulfilled to us their children by raising Jesus, as also it is written in the second Psalm,
>
> "'You are my Son,
> today I have begotten you.'"
> (Acts 13:32–33, quoting Ps. 2:7)

Psalm 2:7 refers to the day that the royal Son of David was "begotten," which in context refers to His accession to the throne. Paul relates this prophetic word to the resurrection of Jesus: The final fulfillment of the accession of the Son of David to the throne comes by means of the resurrection and ascension of Jesus. He is the King who rules finally and fully over the kingdom of David. This is the King to rule over the nations (Ps. 2:8–9) and who will reign over the kingdom forever.

This heavenly exaltation of Christ, therefore, explains to a significant degree the logic of the church's mission in Acts. The Apostolic message is to go from Jerusalem to all Judea and Samaria and even to the end of the earth (Acts 1:8). To a significant degree, this message is that the King of Israel is the resurrected King of the whole world, for the Apostles often emphasize the present glory of Christ in their gospel preaching. Therefore, all people everywhere ought to repent and turn to Him in faith. This is Paul's message to the Athenian Areopagus in Acts 17:30–31:

> "The times of ignorance God overlooked, but now he commands all people everywhere to repent, because he has fixed a day on

> which he will judge the world in righteousness by a man whom he has appointed; and of this he has given assurance to all by raising him from the dead."

No matter where we are from or what we have done, the call is to turn from our sin and turn to Christ, for His kingship is relevant for all people. Only Christ is the eternal Son of God who has taken a human nature in the incarnation, accomplished salvation, and now reigns as the resurrected God-man. There is therefore salvation in no one else, for through faith in Christ we must be saved (see Acts 4:12; 10:36–42).

The message of Acts, therefore, helps us see the relationship of the gospel message to the kingdom of God: Since Jesus is the resurrected Lord of all who will return to judge all people, then we ought to repent and submit to His kingship, whoever we are. The spread of the gospel to all nations therefore follows on the logic of Jesus' resurrection and exaltation to the heavenly throne. He is not just the King for one people, but He reigns from heaven over a kingdom that transcends all earthly kingdoms. All people everywhere, therefore, are called to repentance.

The Future of the Kingdom

When Jesus ascends, the angels tell His disciples that He will come again in the same way that they saw Him depart (Acts 1:10–11). Jesus' ascension into heaven is not the final movement of the kingdom, for the future glory and power of the kingdom that was previewed in the transfiguration will be realized when Jesus returns as King and Judge of all (see Mark 13:26). This is the time of the consummation of the kingdom.

So while Jesus has already brought the kingdom to earth, the kingdom is not yet here in all its fullness. The kingdom will come in all its fullness when Jesus returns to rule over a new heaven and a new earth.

Remarkably, Jesus also points out the role of the Apostles in the new era of the kingdom: "You are those who have stayed with me in my trials, and I assign to you, as my Father assigned to me, a kingdom, that you may eat and drink at my table in my kingdom and sit on thrones judging the twelve tribes of Israel" (Luke 22:28–30; see also Matt. 19:27–28). The kingdom that Jesus assigns to His disciples refers to the Apostles' important role in the coming consummation of the kingdom. The kingdom assigned to them is their privilege in reigning with Christ. Though the Apostles have a unique role, the promise to reign with Christ extends to all disciples of Christ—all those who are "in Christ."[1]

The promise of the kingdom is that just as Christ reigns now and will return to reign forever, so all those who turn to Him in faith will reign with Him (2 Tim. 2:12; see also Rev. 20:6). Let us therefore follow Christ in this age, despite the cost, that we may reign with Him in glory by His grace in the future. His kingdom will have no end (Luke 1:33; 2 Peter 1:11).

Practical Takeaways

1. Not only is Jesus the suffering Messiah, but He is now the ascended, glorious Lord. He is the authoritative King of the world who is going to return soon. We must bow the knee to King Jesus, that we might be part of His kingdom.

1 See, e.g., Ridderbos, *Coming of the Kingdom*, 172, 199, 403–4.

2. Since Jesus is the King for all people, we must tell people about this King. Everyone needs to hear the good news about the kingdom of God. We should therefore take this message throughout the world and support those who take this message faithfully throughout the world.
3. Jesus lives today and is coming again. Jesus is not a dead figure from the past; He is the living Lord of the church. He created us. He knows us. He loves us. He is a King worth serving. His kingdom will continue to grow until the future consummation of the kingdom. Let us therefore come to Him that we may participate in the present and future glory of the kingdom.

16

The Kingdom Today

We've covered a lot of ground in this book. If you've made it this far, then I hope you have a better understanding of what the kingdom of God is and how it applies to us today.

But no doubt there is still more to say, including about how the kingdom of God relates to each of us in our lives. In this final chapter, I want to reflect further on the question of what the kingdom of God means for us today. Indeed, this is one of the most important questions about the kingdom, and many different answers have been given to this question (as we saw in chapter 1). So I want to provide a concise summary of some of what we have seen so far and then tease out a further working definition of the kingdom, with application to our lives today.

The Contours of the Kingdom

The Gospels narrate how Jesus fulfills the promises of the Davidic covenant to rule over an everlasting kingdom. This kingdom comes not by human effort or ingenuity but through the intervention of God in our world. The kingdom starts small and inconspicuously but will continue to grow in this age until its presence cannot be hidden. It will be evident when Jesus returns that He is indeed the King of kings and Lord of lords. The kingdom is already here, but not yet in all its fullness.

As a supernatural work about a suffering and resurrected Messiah, the kingdom calls for faith and repentance. Therefore, the message of the kingdom is not fundamentally different from the message of the gospel—they are two sides of the same coin. To turn to the risen King of kings means turning from our sin. Jesus describes the kingdom in various ways in Matthew, Mark, and Luke, but the Gospel of John clarifies that the kingdom correlates to life. Fullness of life is found in the kingdom of Christ.

Jesus is the King of the kingdom and its focal point. This explains why Jesus can say to the Pharisees during His ministry that the kingdom is present in their midst (Luke 17:20–21)—that is, the kingdom is present in Jesus Himself.

Righteousness is particularly characteristic of the kingdom, and we ought to seek this righteousness as we seek the kingdom (Matt. 6:33). God's law is the righteous standard that guides life in His kingdom. This means, practically, seeking to obey God's law holistically: internally as well as externally and always looking to Christ as the One who fulfills all righteousness. The lives of kingdom citizens are to be marked by righteousness in practice. To be kingdom-minded is to be scrupulously concerned with true holiness according to God's standards. We should think of how this relates to all of life—not just our spiritual life. Since we are integrated people, we are to think of the application of God's kingdom ethics to all our earthly endeavors.

If we want to participate in the eternal kingdom, then we must cultivate growth in grace in this age (2 Peter 1:11). This is not to say that we can earn the kingdom with our actions, for God must grant us the grace of new life. To participate in the kingdom of God means that we must be born again, or born from above (John 3:3). But the call to kingdom living is the call to cultivate righteousness as we follow Christ.

Applying the Kingdom Today

We come now to the "So what?" of our discussion. How should we practically think of the kingdom of God today?

It is crucial to remember the supernatural character of the kingdom and the supernatural message that accompanies the kingdom. The kingdom message is the message about Jesus as King, which therefore calls for faith and repentance. In any application of the kingdom, we must not miss this essential dimension of the kingdom. The kingdom is a supernatural intrusion into our world, and participating in it requires the supernatural gift of new life by faith.

The kingdom is therefore closely associated with the church, which constitutes the people of the kingdom. The kingdom is bigger than the church, but the church is uniquely identified with the kingdom in this age.

The same cannot be said of other institutions. The kingdom of God is not to be identified with any earthly institution, nation, political movement, or noble cause. It is grossly mistaken to usurp the kingdom as though we could use it for our own ends. The kingdom of God is transcendent.

This does not mean, however, that the kingdom cannot influence earthly institutions, governments, causes, and so forth. Indeed, we should hope that the kingdom of God does influence them. The priorities of the kingdom are God's priorities, and we should long to see these priorities manifested and embraced in this age in all realms of life. We may even expect that as the kingdom in this age spreads, the characteristics of the kingdom will spread. And since the people of the kingdom (that is, the people of the church) are engaged in all sorts of endeavors in this world, they should seek to implement the priorities of the kingdom in whatever activity they may be engaged.

In this sense, we should look for evidence of the kingdom's growth everywhere in this world, and citizens of the kingdom should seek to implement these characteristics in any endeavor they participate in. It is good to fight against human trafficking and the spread of destructive drugs, poverty, injustice, and evil in all its forms. It is good for God's people to be fighting on the front lines of such struggles. But this does not mean that the kingdom is to be identified strictly with any of these causes. It also does not mean that the mission of the church is to be identified with any number of noble causes. Instead, the mission of the church is narrower, focusing on worship and making disciples. But the people of the kingdom who gather on Sundays are scattered through the week,[1] and through the scattered people of God the kingdom of God ought to be spread throughout the world. The coming of the kingdom is God's work, but He often works through His people.

The supernatural dimension of the kingdom also means that we cannot neglect or ignore the message of the kingdom and expect it to spread. The kingdom is closely associated with the Word of God. It spreads as the gospel message is spread, and this message is about how sinners come to faith. The kingdom is not present where people are not supernaturally renewed through the gospel. At the same time,

---

1 See DeYoung and Gilbert, *What Is the Mission of the Church?*, 258.

the kingdom may positively affect all sorts of people at some level in this age, even if such people are not themselves citizens of the kingdom. But by spreading kingdom priorities, God's people should also seek to spread the invitation to participate in an everlasting kingdom of righteousness.

I opened with a preliminary definition of *kingdom* from Geerhardus Vos. Now I will venture my own definition of the kingdom, considering what I have argued throughout this book. Perhaps no definition can capture it all, but here is my attempt to sum up the meaning of the kingdom in the Gospels:

> The kingdom of God is the present and future reality that the reign of God in our world is focused on Jesus Christ, the final Son of David, the Seed of the woman, who has come to save His people from their sins and grant them citizenship in an everlasting kingdom. The kingdom magnifies the glory of God and is marked by fullness of life for His people. Though the kingdom often seems to be invisible in this age, it manifests itself already in the renewed people of the kingdom and the comprehensive righteousness cultivated by these kingdom citizens in anticipation of the kingdom's consummation when Christ returns, at which time the kingdom will be gloriously manifest.

Living in the Light of the Kingdom Today

To find fullness of life, we must turn to Christ and become citizens of His kingdom. The kingdom of God is not a passing social movement.

It will not be established by the next election cycle. The kingdom of God is the long-awaited supernatural work of God that outlasts all human institutions.

So we need to ask some pointed questions:

- Are you a citizen of this kingdom?
- Have you turned from your sins in submission to this gracious King?
- If you have done this in the past, do you continue to turn to Him in repentance and submission?
- If you have, are you seeking His righteousness and implementing it in your spheres of influence?
- Are you seeking the integrated holiness that is to characterize members of the kingdom?
- Who sets the priorities for your life? Do you find them in what the surrounding culture approves of and applauds? Or do you listen to the law of God that is to guide the lifestyle of kingdom citizens—even where it stands opposed to the passing spirit of the age?
- Are you seeking to put yourself first, or do you truly believe that the last will be first and the first will be last?
- Where is your hope? Is it in what you have done, or is it in the Savior who grants us eternal life?

Such questions are appropriate for us as we seek to be faithful kingdom citizens.

But let us not miss the good news that should consistently recalibrate our gaze to the King Himself—toward the One who was made low that we may be made whole, toward the One who gave up His life and rose from the dead that we may live and reign with Him forever.

Let us never miss that the message of the kingdom of God is a message of good news about Jesus.

For Further Reading

Crowe, Brandon D. *The Last Adam: A Theology of the Obedient Life of Jesus in the Gospels*. Baker Academic, 2017. Advanced.

Ferguson, Sinclair B. *The Sermon on the Mount: Kingdom Life in a Fallen World*. Banner of Truth, 1987. All levels.

Poythress, Vern S. *The Miracles of Jesus: How the Savior's Mighty Acts Serve as Signs of Redemption*. Crossway, 2016. All levels.

Pratt, Richard L., Jr. *Designed for Dignity: What God Has Made It Possible for You to Be*. 2nd ed. P&R, 2000. All levels.

Ridderbos, Herman N. *The Coming of the Kingdom*. Translated by H. de Jongste. Edited by Raymond O. Zorn. Presbyterian and Reformed, 1962. Advanced.

Schreiner, Patrick. *The Kingdom of God and the Glory of the Cross*. Short Studies in Biblical Theology. Crossway, 2018. All levels.

Vos, Geerhardus. *The Teaching of Jesus Concerning the Kingdom of God and the Church*. 2nd ed. American Tract Society, 1903. Intermediate.

Scripture Index

OLD TESTAMENT

Genesis
1–2 19
1:26–28 19
2:17 54
3 19
3:15 19, 24, 42
3:22 179
15:4 23
38:26 144
49:1 63

Exodus
4:22–23 20

Leviticus
25 58

Deuteronomy
1:31 20
4:30 63
8:5 20
8:5–6 53
14:1–2 20
17 25
17:14–17 20
18:15 99
18:18 99
19 22
21:25 22
32:4–6 20
32:18–20 20
33:29 121–22

Joshua
2:4–14 144

Judges
18:1 21

Ruth
1:16–17 144
4:16–17 144

1 Samuel
8:4–9 22
10:12 98
13:14 22
17 52
24:13 98

2 Samuel
7:8–16 22–23

7:11–12 23
7:12 23
7:13 23
7:14 23
7:16 23
11 144

1 Kings
4:32 98
11 24
16–22 28
22:17 78, 175

2 Kings
17 36
18–19 36
25 37

1 Chronicles
29:11 68

Ezra
1–2 37

Nehemiah
9:15 79

Psalms
1 122
1–72 26
2 24, 26
2:2 138, 165
2:7 50, 191
2:8–9 191
2:10–12 140
2:12 31
8:5 19
9:18 123
10:16 20
20–21 24
20:7–9 21
22 180–81
22:1 180
22:22 181
22:27–28 181
34:6 123
40 25
40:7–8 25
40:12 25
40:17 123
45 24
45:6 25
70:5 123
72 24
72:1 25
72:2 25
72:7 25
72:12 123
73–89 27
78:2 98
86:1 123
89 24
90–106 27
107–50 27
109:22 123
110 24, 168
110:1 25, 161, 167, 168, 176, 190
118 24, 163–64
118:19–25 163
118:25 163
132 24

137 28
137:1 28
145:10–13 90

Ecclesiastes
12:9 98

Isaiah
2:2 63
2:2–3 140–41
7:7–9 41
7:14 41
9:2–7 29–30
9:6 129
11:1–15 50
35:5–7 92
40:1–2 59
40:1–5 56
40:9 59
40:9–11 56–57
42:1–3 51
42:1–9 51
45:1 37
49:1–6 51
50:4–9 51
52:7 57, 59
52:13–53:11 51
53:4 51
53:6–7 157
53:12 51, 157
55:10–13 104–5
60:1–3 44, 141
60:6 57
61 58
61:1–2 57
61:4 58

Jeremiah
5:14–19 174
23:1–6 174
27 37
31:31–34 174
31:32–33 174
31:34 174
31:38 174
50–51 37

Ezekiel
12:22–23 98
17:2 98
17:3–4 108
17:11–15 108
17:19–21 108
17:22–24 108
20:49 98
34:5 78, 175
34:11–16 79
34:23 57

Daniel
2 35
2:21 39
2:28 63
2:44 35, 38
2:44–45 156
4:10–12 107
4:34–35 39
5:18–30 37
5:28–31 37
5:30–31 37
7 8, 35, 156
7:6 38
7:11–12 38

7:13 8, 167, 176
7:13–14 8, 38, 155, 167
7:14 167, 188
8:3–7 37
8:7–14 38
8:20 37
8:22–25 38
11:2 37
11:5–35 38

Hosea
3:5 63

Joel
2:28 63
2:28–32 63

Amos
9:11–12 30, 141

Micah
2:13 94–95
4:1 63
5:2 43, 138
7:5–7 91

Zechariah
13 175
13:7 175

NEW TESTAMENT

Matthew
1:1 40, 41, 54
1:2–17 40
1:3 143
1:5 143
1:6 54, 143
1:11–12 40
1:16 41
1:17 40, 54
1:21 44, 48, 58, 115
1:22–23 41
3:7–9 143
3:11 5, 48
3:14 49
3:15 49, 120
4:1–11 51
4:10–11 53
4:17 116
4:17–22 115
4:23 47
5–7 114, 116
5:1 115
5:3 116, 122, 130
5:3–12 121
5:5 129
5:7 129
5:9 114, 129
5:10 116
5:10–12 129
5:14–16 120
5:17–18 120
5:17–19 120
5:19 120
5:19–20 116
5:20 118, 119, 120
5:21–26 123
5:21–48 123
5:27–30 123
5:39 114
6:9 114
6:9–13 64, 65
6:10 116, 117

6:11 80
6:33 116, 117, 121
7:1 114
7:6 114
7:21–27 116
7:24–27 124
8:10–12 144
8:17 51
9:35 47
9:35–36 78, 175
9:36 57, 137
10–11 84
10:5–7 139
10:5–16 91
10:7–8 91
10:17–22 91
11 94
11:2–19 92
11:3 92
11:5 92, 122
11:11–12 93
11:12 94
12:1–8 24
12:17–21 51
12:28 89, 117
12:31 88–89
12:42 24
13 105
13:24–30 63
13:31–32 106
13:33 108
13:44–46 109
15:1–9 91, 118
16:15–19 152
16:20 155
16:21–23 154, 187
19:24 117
19:27–28 193
19:28 12
20:28 155, 172
21:14–16 164
21:31 117
21:43 117
22:37–38 125
22:37–39 119
22:46 169
23:23 119
24:14 47
26:26–29 173
26:29 173
26:31 175
26:32 176, 187
26:63 176
26:63–65 176
27:11 176
27:27–31 179
27:38 180
27:46 180
28:16–20 187
28:19 145

Mark
1:2–3 48
1:4 48
1:5 48
1:7 86, 88
1:7–8 48
1:8 5
1:10–11 50
1:11 51, 101
1:12 54
1:12–13 51, 88
1:13 54
1:14–15 55, 59

1:21–28 84
1:24 85
1:37–39 74
1:38 60
2:1–12 73
2:5 73
3:11 85
3:21 92
3:22 87, 90
3:22–30 49, 84, 86, 88, 92
3:23 100
3:24 87
3:27 88
3:28 88
3:29 89
3:30 90
3:31–35 92
3:35 92
4 105
4:1–20 103
4:10–12 103–4
4:13–20 103
4:30–32 106
4:33–34 97
5:3–5 85
5:7 85
5:9 85
6:14–29 79
6:31–44 172
6:52 80, 172
7:1–13 145
7:24–30 145
7:31 142
8:1–9 172
8:14–21 80, 172
8:38–9:1 184
9:1 186
9:2–8 185
9:7 101
9:33–37 132
10:31 133
10:45 155, 156, 157, 172
11:8–10 162
12:12 101
12:17 165
12:35–37 168
13:19 103
13:26 192
14:28 187
14:61 176
14:61–62 8, 167
14:62 167, 176
14:63–64 176
15:2 176
15:7 180
15:16–20 179
15:27 180
15:34 180
16:7 187

Luke
1:31–33 42, 131
1:33 193
1:46–47 130
1:46–55 130
1:51–53 130
1:68–75 166
1:69 166
1:71 166
1:72 166
1:74 166
1:77 167
2:8–12 138
2:10 138, 142

2:10–11 58
2:11 138, 190
2:28–32 142
3:16 5
4:1–13 51
4:13 53
4:18 11, 92, 122
4:18–19 57
4:43 58, 60
6:20 122
8:1 58
9:11 78
10:17 89
10:18–19 89
10:19 89
10:29–37 99
10:37 102, 129
11:2–4 64
11:20 89
12:31 110
12:31–32 111
12:32 110
14:11 133
16:16 58, 94
17 9
17:20–21 9, 10, 12, 60,196
18:17 110, 133
18:18–30 110
19:38 162
22:28–30 12, 193
22:37 51
22:66 176
22:67 176
23:2 177
23:3 176
24:50–51 189

John
3:3 197
3:16 75
6:15 79
6:33–40 79
6:56 79
8:34–36 88
10:10 75
10:17–18 76, 169, 175, 187
11 76
18:1–3 175
18:9 175
18:10–11 178
18:33–37 177
18:40 180
19:1–5 179
19:5 179
19:7–9 178
19:10 178
19:11 178
19:15 178
19:19 180
20:30–31 77

Acts
1:8 143
1:10–11 192
2:17 63
2:17–21 63
2:23 178
2:25–28 190
2:29–36 189–90
2:36 143
4:11 164
4:12 192
4:19 165
5:29 165

10:36 58
10:36–42 192
10:38 50
13:32–33 191
17:30–31 191

Romans
1:16 139
3:23 55
5:12–21 169
5:18 55

1 Corinthians
1:18–25 134
11:26 173
15:17 184
15:21 169
15:54–57 184

Ephesians
2:12 148
2:13 148
2:19–20 148

Colossians
1:13–14 89

1 Timothy
2:1–2 170

2 Timothy
2:12 193

Titus
2:13–14 169

Hebrews
1:8 25
2:12 181
10:5–10 25

James
1:8 125
1:9–10 131
2:1–13 134
2:5 11, 131
2:13 129
2:25 144
4:8 125
5:13–16 73

1 Peter
1:10–12 158
2:7 164
2:13–17 170
2:19–23 181
5:8 67

2 Peter
1:11 193, 196
1:16–18 186

1 John
3:8 13, 83, 167

Revelation
17:14 188
20:6 193

OLD TESTAMENT PSEUDEPIGRAPHA

Psalms of Solomon
17:21–22 153

About the Author

Dr. Brandon D. Crowe is professor of New Testament at Westminster Theological Seminary in Philadelphia. He is also the author of *The Lord Jesus Christ*, *Why Did Jesus Live a Perfect Life?*, and *The Path of Faith*.